The Last Word on
Lutefisk

Cod drying on outdoor racks in Norway.

The Last Word on
Lutefisk

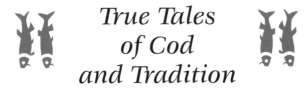

*True Tales
of Cod
and Tradition*

GARY LEGWOLD

CONRAD HENRY PRESS
MINNEAPOLIS

The Last Word on Lutefisk
True Tales of Cod and Tradition

By Gary Legwold

Published by:
Conrad Henry Press
5205 Knox Avenue South
Minneapolis, MN 55419-1041
1-888-LUTEFIS = 1-888-588-3347 (toll free)
Web site: http://www.lutefisk.com
E-mail: glegwold@lutefisk.com

ISBN 0-9652027-0-4
Library of Congress Catalog Card Number: 96-77791.

The following lyrics, poems, and humor used with permission of their authors or editors: p. 21 and 126, jokes, and p. 129, "O Lutefisk" from Red Stangland's *Norwegian Home Companion*; p. 78, lutefisk definition, and p. 120, letter-to-the-editor response from the *Western Viking*, Oct. 27, 1995; p. 125, humor from *Lute Koubason's Lutefisk Handbook*, by Bob Fredell; p. 126 joke from *The Best of Queen Lena*, by Charlene Power; p. 126–127, jokes from *101 More Things to Do With Lutefisk*, by Ed Fischer; p. 128, "Love That Lutefisk" from *Leftover Lutefisk* by Art Lee; p. 130, selected lyrics from "I Want To Go Where The Wild Goose Goes" from *Cold, Cold Heart (and other 'TORCH' songs)* by Doug Setterberg and Stan Boreson; p. 130–131, selected stanzas from "Lutefisk Lament" by Don Freeburg (for copies of the entire poem, send $1.50 to Freeburg at 7201 York Ave. S., Minneapolis, MN 55435); p. 132, "Lutefisk March" by Robert G. Olson; p. 136–137, humor from Bill Wundram of the *Quad-City Times*; p. 137, humor by George Hesselberg of the *Wisconsin State Journal*; and p. 148, humor from *Lake Wobegon Days*, reprinted by permission of Garrison Keillor, copyright © 1985 Garrison Keillor.

Book design by Will Powers. Cover design by Don Leeper.
Typesetting by Stanton Publication Services, Inc., St. Paul.

Dedication

To Mom,
To Dad,
To Uncle Cliff.

They stroll in the place
Where there is no if.

All is yes.

Acknowledgments

Tusen takk to Liv Dahl and John Hogenson at the Sons of Norway. They gave me lutefisk leads other than "follow your nose."

Thanks to the determined folks who worked on The Lutefisk Dinner Directory. They are Arvid Weflen (Alaska), Audun Toven (Washington), Vi and Jeannie Obert (Montana and Canada), Dawn Morgan (North Dakota and northern Minnesota), Tami Bengtson (northern Minnesota), Doris Nesthus (South Dakota), Eunice Stoen (Iowa), Jon and Jane Grinde (Wisconsin), and Cathy Mix (everywhere else). A special thanks to Kim Venuta who did southern Minnesota and organized the directory so well.

A book is only as good as its cover, so a deep bow to Bitten Norvoll, who helped make the cover just right. And, of course, to Randi Unstad, who never looked finer.

To my good friends Earl Hipp, Dave Kamminga, Cris Anderson, Tom Eckstein, Richard Mraz, and Dick Wilson—thanks for getting me off the dime and for keeping me rolling. And to you, Rick Naymark, for editing the lutefisk poetry. May you learn to love lutefisk as well as you love mountain climbing.

Susan McCallum, you were the safety net. Who else would catch the misspelling of Allis-Chalmers? Cathy Mix, thanks for one last read-through and making one computer talk to the other. The world is a nicer place when we talk.

Finally, a heartfelt thanks to Kathy Weflen. She was in there all the way, editing the book, making good writing better. In tennis you don't get better unless the ball comes back. The same is so with writing. Kathy sent back my drafts, but I always knew we were on the same side.

Photograph and illustration credits

p. 15 illustration courtesy of the Norwegian Seafood Export Council

p. 21 illustration by Ed Fischer

p. 24 historic photos by unknown photographer, courtesy of Olsen Fish Co. in Minneapolis

p. 27 illustration by Kaare Espolin Johnson, courtesy of Gisle Espolin Johnson, Oslo, Norway

p. 29 historic photos by unknown photographer, courtesy of Olsen Fish Co. in Minneapolis

p. 33 map produced with the permission and assistance of Destination Lofoten, Svolvær, Norway

p. 54 historic photo by unknown photographer, courtesy of Olsen Fish Co. in Minneapolis

p. 55 historic photo by unknown photographer, courtesy of Olsen Fish Co. in Minneapolis

p. 58 historic photos by unknown photographer, courtesy of Olsen Fish Co. in Minneapolis

p. 62 photo by David H. Andreae

p. 83 illustration by Ed Fischer

p. 93 photo by Bruno of Hollywood, NYC

p. 98 photo: *St. Paul Daily News,* Minnesota Historical Society

p. 100 photo courtesy of Emma Vatn

p. 119 illustration by Ed Fischer

p. 124 illustration by Les Kouba

p. 127 illustration by Ed Fischer

p. 139 illustration by Ed Fischer

p. 142 illustration by Ed Fischer

p. 160 photo by Darroll Bengtson

p. 165 photo courtesy of Henry Schumacher

p. 170 photos courtesy of Marilyn Legwold

Contents

The Last Word on
Lutefisk

1

A Night at the Lutefisk Opera

Lutefisk is a lead-in.

Lutefisk is not easy to love, or even like. What's more, it's not easy to explain to the uninitiated. But here goes. Lutefisk is fish (cod or ling) that has been preserved by drying. This hardened stockfish is prepared for cooking by soaking it for several weeks first in water, then in a lye solution (that's right), and finally in water again. The term *lutefisk* comes from the Norwegian, *lute,* meaning to wash in lye solution, and *fisk,* meaning fish. The Swedish term is *lutfisk,* Danish *ludefisk.*

The result of drying, soaking, and boning is a translucent, gel-like meat you can boil or bake. Lutefisk's subtle taste will not offend you, but the odor probably will.

So, I repeat: Lutefisk, what with the lye bath and the legendary odor, is not easy to love. Of course, the same can be said about opera: It is not easy to love. Opera lovers may sputter and blanche at the very notion of comparing this lofty art to the lowly lutefisk. But hear me out.

When you attend your first opera, you are likely to wonder what opera-goers see in this. All the incessant singing in Italian or German. Why don't they just say it, and in plain English? And the singing, except for the big arias, might strike the new listener as melodramatic, shrieky, pompous, and at times one-note. The stories are often boy meets girl, and the two become involved in messy tragedies, rife with half-drunk poets, obsessive noblemen, wrathful women, and villains who prey on good people cursed with bad judgment. Humorist Ed Gardner said, "Opera is when a guy gets stabbed in the back and, instead of bleeding, he sings."

If Gardner were speaking about lutefisk, he might say, "Lutefisk is when a guy holds his nose to eat lye-laced fish and, instead of gagging, he grins."

Lutefisk, like opera, rewards suffering and perseverance. If you stay with opera—give it a chance to enter your heart—you can grow to love the passion, spectacle, and soaring voices. If you stay with lutefisk—give it a chance to get into your heart and maybe even your taste buds—an evening of savoring this simple meal will be as good as a night at the opera. Indeed, for some of us who have long lived under the influence of trace levels of lye, a church basement full of Lutherans singing the praises of lutefisk *is* an opera.

Of course, the passion and the spectacle of a lutefisk dinner are not as obvious as with opera, but this you would expect with something so Scandinavian. And the story is not boy meets girl, although in the last decade in Norway, a bold, against-the-grain advertising campaign presented lutefisk as an aphrodisiac. Surprisingly, sales soared and lutefisk lovers' clubs were founded. An American interpreter, who prefers to remain anonymous, fears a churchgoers backlash if and when this campaign hits the New World. Dismissively, he boiled the campaign down to this: "Eat lutefisk today, get lucky tonight."

Despite the rarity of romantic encounters at lutefisk dinners in North America, some of the characters you

*A bold, Norwegian and Swedish advertising campaign
proclaimed "Lutefisk lovers: Love tonight." Ads hinted that
lutefisk lovers make better lovers.*

find there are as colorful and heroic, in their quiet way,
as any you'll find in Mozart's *Don Giovanni*—and they
are real.

Aria in Beldenville

Like an opera, a lutefisk dinner is full of anticipation, a
build-up to the climactic scene. Consider, for example, one
of the first lutefisk dinners I attended. After driving an
hour and a half southeast of Minneapolis to Beldenville,
Wis., I could not find Our Savior's Lutheran Church, site
of the annual lutefisk event. So I stopped at a bar and
asked a patron for directions. He gave me a look and then
shouted across the bar to the proprietor that I was looking
for some lutefisk dinner. Heads turned my way, and the
bar owner crossed the room. He smiled and pointed me in
the right direction.

I drove into the countryside. It was now 7:30 p.m. and October's darkness had long since descended. After about five miles, I saw a cluster of lights brightening the horizon. I drove closer, suddenly feeling hungry. Across the cornfield I could see tall pines catching the glow from high, arching church windows. This had to be the place, I thought.

A small sign posted near the driveway gave notice of the lutefisk dinner. I wondered if the parishioners debated every year whether the small sign was really necessary. A man with a flashlight pointed my car to a vacated spot in the matted-grass parking lot.

I stepped out of the car into the clear night air. Through open kitchen windows, I could hear the behind-the-scenes clatter and tings and high-pitched conversation that go with serving church food and washing dishes. I entered the church and paid $9 for ticket number 1140—that many people had already bought tickets, I was told, many of them arriving that afternoon in yellow buses.

I waited in the sanctuary for my turn to eat, thinking about how these people must really love lutefisk to temporarily alter the sanctity of their place of worship with lutefisk's aroma. Of course, medieval cathedrals sheltered sheep and pigs, setting the precedent that prayer could not be diminished—perhaps it could even be enhanced—by earthy odors. (Come to think of it, I wonder what's the origin of the word "*pew?*")

After five minutes or so, the ticket seller called number 1140 along with several others. This person appeared to be pleasant and accommodating. I wondered if the job demanded someone naturally gifted at calming the normally friendly folks who, during waits that sometimes last an hour or two, feel they can no longer tolerate the tease of being so close to lutefisk and yet so far. (I imagined a head-

Lutefisk dinners pack 'em in.
This one at Mount Olivet Lutheran Church in Minneapolis
usually feeds nearly 1,800 people in four hours.

line: "Seething Scandinavians Storm Sanctuary.") However, with only a short wait tonight, there was no risk of a mob scene. I rose from my pew and lined up with a dozen other lutefisk devotees. As we wound our way down the dim stairs to the basement, a merry din came up at us, as did the ever stronger fish odor.

We turned a corner into the basement all abuzz. Women in bright red Norwegian costume dresses called *bunads* were whizzing to and fro, whirling around table ends to serve more Swedish meatballs here, more lefse there. Other women were seating people at the 30 or so tables, covered with simple tablecloths and arranged in a way that made the large room seem intimate. Smiling women swerved around whitewashed floor-to-ceiling poles, gracefully swooping up empty platters, stooping to pour coffee, and squeezing through the passages between tables and paneled walls decorated with garlands and posters of scenes from the old country.

A woman in a *bunad* beckoned me and a few others to an open table. No sooner did we unfold our napkins and nod to our neighbors, when presto, another woman presented a platter heaped with steaming, shimmering lutefisk. Ah, let the feast begin! I took my first bite. Mmmmm. Indeed, this was the big aria. Fabulous fish. Firm, flaky morsels melted in my mouth.

Bowls were passed and refills requested. Diners at my table seemed content to quietly savor the meal and not distract themselves with small talk. What talk there was was all to the point: Sugar please. Certainly. Could I trouble you for some flatbread? *Tusen takk* (a thousand thanks in Norwegian). Care for cole slaw, or a roll? I'll take some melted butter for my lutefisk, please. Pass the cream sauce, if you would. Gee, I don't know if I have room on my plate for meatballs. Oh, I'll pile them on the potatoes. The lefse, I almost forgot about that. Please pass the butter and sugar. Yes, just a little more lutefisk, thanks. It is good this year, the fish. Coffee would be fine, thanks. I better save room for those *sandbakkels* (pastries) and *krumkake* (small cones) I see over there. I'm sure I won't have room for the *rømmegrøt* (cream pudding).

I finished and pushed my chair back from the table, amazed at how much I'd eaten of such simple fare. No secret spice mixture, no rich red sauces that dominated the palate. But such taste. I realized, with some surprise, that a plain potato—no butter, no sour cream—actually had flavor. Same with a roll. And the lutefisk? It was prepared to perfection, not overcooked to wallpaper-paste consistency. And it was flavorful; don't let anyone tell you lutefisk is tasteless. The flavor is subtle—fishy, to be sure—and cannot be separated from its slide-down-the-throat texture and rich Scandinavian tradition. But it does have flavor. I doubt that lutefisk alone has enough flavor to attract hundreds of paying customers. However, when served with side dishes of more common foods, lutefisk takes center stage and draws a crowd. A lutefisk dinner is a classic case of the whole being greater than the sum of the parts.

I rose from the table and began making my way out. I met Norma Taplin, one of the women wearing a *bunad*, and she introduced me to Audrey Halverson, Gehart Iverson, LeMoine Christopherson, and several others. They were taking down wall decorations, cleaning up in the kitchen, and straightening the dining room. For the most part, these were people near or past retirement age. A night like this had to be exhausting, and a few folks I talked with wondered aloud just how long these dinners can keep going. But most people, instead of being depleted by the day, seemed to be buoyed; beat yet upbeat.

I asked Rev. Richard Ulvilden, the Norwegian-American pastor who had recently retired, "What is it about lutefisk dinners that energizes and unites a community?"

He paused, leaned back in his folding chair, and put his hands behind his head. Finally, he looked me in the eye and gave me the answer: "Lutefisk, the cod that passes all understanding."

Amen.

From Lefse to Lutefisk

Four years ago I wrote *The Last Word on Lefse*. Since then, events have happened in my life that I could never have foreseen. In the Nordic Fest parade in Decorah, Iowa, I rode in a red convertible as author of a lefse book. I have spoken at Sons of Norway lodge meetings, taught community education classes on lefse making, demonstrated lefse making at book signings and at Ingebretsen's (a Scandinavian market in Minneapolis), given lengthy interviews on radio talk shows, and heard countless confessions of wannabe lefse makers who have gained inspiration and confidence from my book. Newspapers and magazines have been kind with their features and reviews, and I have signed books at the Norsk Høstfest in Minot, N.D., the Scandinavian Hjemkomst Festival in Fargo, N.D., Lefse Dagen in Starbuck, Minn., Syttende Mai in Benson, Minn., and Norway Days and other fests in Minneapolis.

Lefse has led me many places, and now it has led me to lutefisk. This was not a planned stop. It was as if lefse, my first love in the world of Norwegian-American cooking, took me home to her family. There I met lutefisk, her peculiar, sometimes princely, sometimes profane uncle. How did lefse, a delicate, doily-like flatbread with pretty brown spots and a delicious taste, ever get such kooky kin as a lye-soaked fish? The answer, I once thought, was displayed on a T-shirt I created and wear when I do public appearances. It says:

LEFSE
An Antidote For Lutefisk

Ah, the fun we poke at lutefisk. There's the old joke about skunks taking up residence under the porch. A neighbor tells the homeowner that the surest way to evict them is to pitch lutefisk under there. The homeowner does just that. The neighbor is glad to hear the skunks have cleared out but is stumped when the homeowner asks, "Now, how the heck do I get rid of the Norwegians under the porch?"

Then there's the one Roger Erickson told one morning on WCCO radio in Minneapolis. It seems that lutefisk was responsible for the famous runestone "discovered" in northern Minnesota. When the Vikings arrived they leaned their lutefisk against this rock, which of course *ruined* the stone.

And the irrepressible, often ribald Red Stangland could not restrain himself when he wrote about lutefisk in his many humor books. As an example, it seems that Ole and Lena once had the Torkelsons over for lutefisk and lefse. Their guests liked butter and pepper on their lutefisk, but Lena couldn't find the pepper. She rummaged around in the cupboard and found a container she thought was pepper. Turns out, it was gunpowder. So the next day Ole called Torkelson and told him of the mistake. "Vell, I'm glad to find out vhat happened," said Torkelson, "becoss vhen ve got home last night, I leaned over to tie my shoe and I accidentally shot da cat."

This is not great humor. Some might not call it humor at all. But with lutefisk, this buffoonery is as inescapable as the smell. Go to any lutefisk dinner and sooner or later someone around you will take a good-natured poke at lutefisk. This leads to a repartee of jokes and one-liners and rejoinders, punctuated by red-faced guffaws and "uff-da" head shaking.

Some Scandinavian-Americans detest this. They feel that people get hung up on the smell and the humor and never get to the meat of the matter—that lutefisk is an important food for Scandinavians and, when properly prepared, makes for a delectable meal. That said, most Scandinavians roll with the humor. They anticipate and relish it and would be disappointed if a gag order on lutefisk humor were imposed.

The humor pulls them in, huddles them together, invites rapt attention, and sometimes flushes out the not-so-reluctant ham in all of them. The humor warms the dining hall and stirs memories of Christmas eves when the same jokes were told over lutefisk and lefse. And frankly, the lutefisk humor, as rank is it can become, is about the only agent powerful enough to penetrate the stoicism of oh, so many Scandinavians.

A common response from Scandinavian-Americans to *The Last Word on Lefse* is the same one I have already heard about *The Last Word on Lutefisk:* "How can you write so much about so little?" My answer: The lefse book was not just about lefse. The book was about the people who make, eat, and cherish lefse—lefse legends like 91-year-old Ida Sacquitne, who made lefse at the Smithsonian Institution and for the King of Norway; newsmakers like Anna Alden, who made lefse on roller skates; the Boys of Starbuck, who made the world's largest lefse (9 feet 8 inches across); salesmen like Carl Knutson, who drove around the Midwest fiddling, making up lefse songs, and selling lefse; and historians like Torbjorn Norvoll, who recounted how his Norwegian hometown survived on potatoes and lefse during German occupation in World War II.

When I turned my attention to lutefisk, I sought out notable lutefisk fanciers who frequented the hundreds of lutefisk dinners in Minnesota, Wisconsin, Iowa, North

Dakota, South Dakota, and the state of Washington. My quest led me to 93-year-old Obert Anderson, who told me about the old days when small lutefisk processing companies popped up on just about every street corner in Minneapolis. I met Uncle Torvald, who at one time teamed up with Red Stangland to form a vaudeville act of Scandinavian humor. And I met Ellen Repp, who once ran for governor of Washington on the "Lutefisk Party ticket." In the following chapters, you'll learn more about this cast of lutefisk-loving characters.

Naturally, my lutefisk research led me to Norway, where I caught cod in March near the Lofoten Islands, which are north of the Arctic Circle. I saw how those fisheries work, then visited the lutefisk processing plants here in the United States. I learned from one Norwegian-born American, Odd Unstad, the old-country way of making lutefisk at home. A self-taught lutefisk gourmet, Odd cooks heavenly cod. You will find out how to make it his way.

If you would rather eat lutefisk than read about it, go immediately to The Lutefisk Dinner Directory at the back of the book. It lists most of the lutefisk dinners in North America, by state and by date. With the help of this directory, you can follow your appetite (or your nose), from Texas to Alaska. Who knows, maybe you can organize your own lutefisk tour.

Whatever you take from *The Last Word on Lutefisk*— the humor, how-to, stories—keep in mind that lutefisk, like lefse, is only a lead-in to the big show: the people. Lutefisk devotees are "real characters," as my mom used to say. They will jolt you with their jokes, warm you with kindness, and inspire you with unassuming nobility.

Early 1940s photos show the history of lutefisk.
For centuries fishermen on Norway's beautiful Lofoten Islands
have caught and hung cod. The cod dry to become stockfish,
which eventually becomes lutefisk.

2

The Lofotens

Lutefisk begins on these northern Norwegian islands.

The prop plane dipped suddenly and everyone aboard let out an involuntary "Whoooa!" The plane steadied, shivered a bit, then shuddered and dipped again. Passengers cranked their heads from side to side, trying to gain some assurance from the view out the cabin windows. All we could see was snow white—a blank screen that my imagination filled with worst-case scenarios.

I was on a Norwegian airline flight that makes the 150-mile hop from Bodø in northern Norway, over the Vestfjord waters to Svolvær, the central city of the Lofoten Islands. The Lofotens are a mountainous, high-shouldered wall of weather-moody islands about 100 miles north of the Arctic Circle. For centuries this archipelago of about 80 small islands with some 24,000 inhabitants has been famous for cod fishing. This is where the story of lutefisk begins.

The month was March, and fishing was in full swing. I reminded myself that a snowstorm was not unusual for the season. Over the high-pitched, urgent drone of the engines, the captain announced that Svolvær was socked in. Jiggling passengers strained to listen: Maybe we could land in

Leknes, a couple of islands to the south. Otherwise, back to Bodø.

I looked around the small cabin, which was nearly full with about 20 tourists arriving for the fishing season. A French couple sat across the aisle from me, but I surmised from overheard conversations that most of the travelers were Norwegians. People were either thin-lipped and jaw-set, or they wore the universal mask of false bravery—smile fixed on the mouth and panic in the eyes.

I imagined the stunning Lofoten mountains I had seen in pictures and wondered about our chances of slamming into one of them. Or plunging into the Vestfjord, our engines freezing up and sputtering during descent. The clouds parted for a moment, and I spotted a fishing boat. We were not that far above the water. If a couple of key bolts fail, I thought, we could be in the drink in a moment. Well, at least the fishing boat was close by. Could it reach us before hypothermia set in?

I had to get a grip on myself. We flew south for a relatively uneventful 10 minutes. The captain announced that we had been cleared for landing at Leknes. The news was greeted by a collective sigh. We touched down once on the snowy runway then rolled toward the small terminal. When the pilot cut the engines, the sound effect was that of the plane collapsing in exhaustion. I was on the Lofotens, safe and sound and a bit shaky.

After I collected my bags, I boarded a bus for the 70-kilometer ride northeast to Svolvær, where I would stay for four days. As the bus rolled onto highway E10 (a.k.a. King Olav Road), I realized I was bushed. I had visited relatives in Seljord, in the Telemark region, and then did a three-day sauna tour in southern Finland. The heat from the bus was delicious as driving snow and sleet pecked at the tall windows. The bus ride rocked me, and try as I might to take in the gray, gauzy mountains and ocean, I fell asleep.

Centuries of Cod

When I awoke, I read about the Lofotens. Documents dating back to around the year 900 AD show that boats from

Himmelskipet (The Heavenly Ship)
This black-and-white lithograph, by Lofoten Island artist Kaare Espolin Johnson, depicts how men once braved rough water in open rowboats just to reach the bounteous Lofoten winter fisheries.

along Norway's northwest coast have always traveled to the Lofotens for the winter cod-fishing season. From January through April, teeming shoals of cod sweep down from the Barents Sea to spawn in the Lofoten's plankton-rich waters. While fishing was good along much of the Norwegian coast, tales of the extremely bounteous winter fisheries off the Lofotens lured fishermen. For days and weeks, the men braved rough water in open rowboats and sailboats.

The Lofoten fisheries peaked around the time of World War II, when 20,000 to 25,000 fishermen converged there. The men stayed in seaside shanties, each shanty called a *rorbu*. Øystein, Norway's King in 1120, ordered construction of the first *rorbus* in Lofoten. It was a nod to the importance of fishing to the country's economy even back then. Before *rorbus*, fishermen simply slept beneath boats overturned on shore.

In a *rorbu* made of cogged timber, often on poles in the sea, a fishing crew of eight to 20 men slept, cooked, repaired tackle, and baited long lines. Each fisherman kept a chest with his clothing and some lefse, flatbread, and other food. Today, 200 to 300 *rorbus* still stand, and tourists often rent them.

Since World War II, fishing, while still good most years, has declined. The peak was 1948, when the Lofoten catch was 148,000 tons of cod, says Rolf Jentoft, whose family has been in the Lofoten fishing business for five generations. In 1995 the catch was 35,000 tons, about average for the last 10 years. Quotas, established in 1990, have helped prevent further decline due to overfishing. Each boat is allowed to catch a certain tonnage, set by boat length. For example, a standard $800,000 50-foot boat (boats vary between 20 and 100 feet) is allowed 150 tons of whole fish per year, or 100 tons of headed and gutted fish.

Today, about 3,000 fishermen work the Lofoten waters.

Bringing in the cod.
*The peak years for Lofoten fishing were the 1940s,
when 20,000 to 25,000 fishermen converged on the islands.
These photos of that era show men hauling in the catch (top)
and then bleeding fish on shore at day's end (bottom).*

About half of them reside on the islands. The rest come from all parts of the Norwegian coast, most of them sleeping on board their modern fishing vessels. A good day's catch may equal 10 tons. After the Lofoten cod season ends, they fish along Norway's coast and out at sea, netting more cod, haddock, herring, ling, and other fish. They work six days a week and about 320 days a year.

The catch is always too plentiful to be eaten fresh and is therefore preserved. In other parts of Norway some fish are kiln-dried in a matter of days. In the Lofotens, however, all the cod are dried naturally on wooden racks in the open air from February to April or May. The dried fish are called stockfish.

I have been told that what France is to grapes, the Lofotens are to stockfish. That is, the Gulf Stream that courses through the Lofotens creates a climate perfect for drying stockfish: not too warm, which would cause rotting, and not too cold, which would cause freezing. Supposedly, the dried fish lose only the water and none of the nutritional value. Rolf Jentoft tells me the weight of the dried fish is reduced to 23 percent of the weight of the fresh fish.

Beginning in May each year, the stockfish is exported. As early as 874 AD, Norwegians traded this hard-as-wood stockfish to England and Western Europe in exchange for grain, honey, and cloth. What fish they didn't trade they stacked floor to ceiling in sheds. The stockfish served both as a dietary staple and a means of paying taxes.

In her fine book, *Lutefisk, Rakefisk and Herring in Norwegian Tradition,* Astri Riddervold says that at one time Norwegians ate stockfish instead of bread. She refers to letters written around 1431 by an Italian aristocrat, Querini, who wintered on the northern coast of Norway because of a shipwreck. He described how people beat the hard, dry stockfish with a hammer until almost a powder. Then they mixed it with butter and seasoning, and ate it raw.

Today, most of the stockfish is exported. If, for example, the total finished product amounts to 4,000 tons, Rolf says, only 500 tons stay in Norway to make lutefisk for Norwegians. The rest of the stockfish is exported directly from the Lofotens. Much of it goes to Italy, where it is soaked in water and cooked in a variety of recipes that call for oil, wine, tomatoes, onions, and spices.

Until the 1980s some of the Lofoten stockfish was marked for the United States, where it was processed into lutefisk. Today, says Jentoft, the cod that goes to the United States amounts to "peanuts." U.S. lutefisk processors have switched from cod to ling, a cousin to cod. Why? Ling, which is not a significant part of the Lofoten catch, is cheaper. More on this later.

None of the cod goes to waste. The heads are sold to African countries to be ground into flour. The tongues are cut out and sold separately as a delicacy. The roe becomes caviar. The liver is used for cod liver oil. Carcass parts go to South American fertilizer factories.

Riddervold writes that lutefisk is first mentioned around 1536 in history books by Olaus Magnus. He described how lutefisk was prepared in strong lye, rinsed, and boiled for eating. Variations of this method of preparation have been described ever since by Norwegian, Swedish, and Finnish sources. When Scandinavian immigrants arrived on American shores starting in the 19th century, they brought with them the lutefisk tradition. That tradition survives in the United States, Canada, and Scandinavia.

The Light of the Lofotens

The bus pulled into the small Svolvær airport. I picked up my Avis rental car, drove into Svolvær, and parked on the narrow street in front of Hotel Havly. This old hotel has been a seaman's mission. *Havly* means sea shelter. Ballstad, Stamsund, and a few other fishing towns on the islands have a Hotel Havly, where fishermen can sleep, shower, eat, and socialize. However, the guests at this Havly appeared to be mostly tourists who, if they were like me, found the simple accommodations charming and the staff down-home and hospitable.

My room on the third floor overlooked the street entrance. The bed was firm and was across the spacious room from a couch and desk. A broad window showed a flurry of snow. I looked down at the snowflakes lighting on the heads and shoulders of pedestrians. A biker, head hunched over handlebars, noodled through the slush, laboring in a low gear (but probably loving every minute of it). Several blocks away was the dock where two nights later I would witness the unloading of the ferry from Bodø.

It was late afternoon and I decided to take a walk around this town of about 4,000 people. Plows were pushing snow into the sea, chunks of white dissolving into black. I stopped at the ferry dock to take a picture of the Svolvær Goat, two famous horn-like rock columns on a nearby mountain. I had seen travel brochure photos of a roped-up rock climber jumping from one horn to the other. Though I am a rock climber, the slippery old Goat did not tempt me on this snowy day.

I tromped into one of many art galleries in town. There I first saw the legendary Lofotens in paintings. Tor Dahl, a Norwegian friend back in Minneapolis, had told me that the Lofotens are an artists' center. The breathtaking contrast of mountains against ocean and the colorful fishing images attract painters, he said. But mostly the artists come for the light. The Lofotens are in darkness for several weeks before and after Christmas. When the light returns, it is beyond description, artists claim.

When I left the gallery, the light had left for the day, but my appetite had not. So I hoofed it over to the Royal Hotel Lofoten for cod tongue and a beer. Supposedly a delicacy, the cod tongue was breaded, fried, and greasy. I told myself

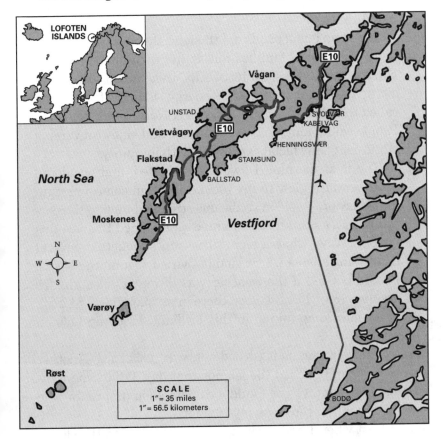

it was probably like lutefisk: You have to acquire a taste for it. I finished my salad, potatoes, bread, and beer, and walked back to my room.

At Hotel Havly the staff was handing out candles to the guests, who lingered in the lobby or dining room. Power outage, they explained. The next day the newspaper, *Lofotposten*, led with a headline: "Lofoten stoppet." An avalanche had snapped a main power line, leaving all of the Lofotens without electricity. This explained why I dined in candlelight and why on my walk back I had noticed the nostalgic glow of candles in all the shops, bars, and restaurants.

If we run out of candles, I thought, then we can pass the night as Lofoten families did at the turn of the century. During the sunless winter weeks, they would sometimes sit in darkness to conserve energy. Erling H. Peterson called this *sitte skjøming* in his book *Hang on the Potatoes*. People would knit, sing hymns, pray, and enjoy conversing while using any facial expression with impunity.

The next morning I awoke disoriented, and wondered about a weird glow in my room. Fire from someone's candle? Hazy gray-golden sunbeams streamed though the partially drawn curtains. I squinted as I opened the curtains farther. Wow, what a sight! The sun silhouetted several mountains offshore. Low clouds swirled around the peaks. I could not tell if the weather was lifting or reloading for another arctic blast. I stood there in my pajamas for I don't know how long, taking in this brilliant, brooding Lofoten nimbus.

The weather, as it turned out, was not lifting. Another snowstorm pounded the islands that day. I did some writing and reading, and found a camera shop proprietor who made a minor repair on my Olympus.

Just when I had given up on shooting slides, the clouds

cruised away in formation, riding low over the water and out to sea. Stunned by this Lofoten aura, I hopped in my car and spent the eventide driving a few kilometers south on the eastern shoreline and photographing freely. The sun flared as it reached the horizon, a nozzle of orange spray against a wet, blue ballroom floor.

All else that day was a quiet epilogue. Memories of the Lofoten light dominated my mind's eye as I closed my eyes to sleep.

The Cod Kisser

The next morning I popped out of bed, hoping for the same glow I had seen the previous morning. Nope. More snow. And today was the day I was booked to go cod fishing. Would we still go?

I dressed and ate and walked to the tourist information center, where an old whaling vessel was to pick up paying passengers who wanted to land a cod or two. Yes, I was told, we will fish today.

The white, 80-foot whaler arrived, and about 10 men and women boarded and stowed gear in the heated cabin. The vessel chugged toward our destination about six miles out. Conditions were cold and gray and, I was told, calm. Yet the boat bucked slowly up and down, and the deck's angle became alarmingly steep at times.

We reached a fishing spot, and our engines were cut. Clouds covered the mountains, but we could still see the shore. We were the only tourist boat among the eight smaller fishing boats, most of them 50-footers.

Fishermen wearing orange rubber bib overalls were dropping or hauling in nets, 3 to 4 yards wide and 30 to 35 yards long. The fishing crews lower the weighted nets 50 to 180 yards. Sonars help them determine that depth. They buoy the nets to keep them at a chosen depth. When the fishermen haul in the nets later in the day, they immediately bleed the fish by cutting the major blood vessels in the neck. They store the bloodless fish in bins of ice water.

Crews also catch fish on what they call a long line. The line, up to 900 yards long, has baited hooks every nine feet. The boat carries up to 10 bins of long lines (one per bin), which the men set one day and haul in the next.

One of our guides announced it was time to catch cod. A few passengers who had their own gear began casting. The rest of us took turns at the tire-sized reels on posts bolted to the deck. Following the guide's instructions, I lowered a shiny artificial lure (maybe 9 inches long, with several hooks) about 100 yards down, and tried to attract the fish by grabbing the line and raising my hand overhead, in a 5-o'clock-to-1-o'clock arc.

After several minutes of line lifting, I thought I felt resistance. "I've got something!" I yelled. I started cranking furiously on the reel but was quickly told to slow down and reel in steadily. Suddenly, the line went limp. Ah, the one that got away, I thought.

Another person took my spot while I took photos and ate lunch. I had eaten just a couple of bites of my sandwich when a man from Stavanger, Norway, started reeling in earnest. Soon he had landed the first catch of the day.

Other anglers became discouraged and tired. Their line-lifting began to look less like fishing and more like waving a flag in surrender. I took my turn again, and bingo! I had one on the line. This time I steadily reeled in the line. There was hardly any fight to this fish, I thought, and soon the Stavanger man reached into the water with the gaff, and up came the brown-green cod with its distinctive lateral lines. Man, was I excited!

I wondered how many lutefisk meals it would make. Eight? Ten? It was an average cod, as cods go; most are around 9 pounds, and a few reach 100 pounds. But it was the biggest fish I had ever caught. I was roundly congratulated, and everyone joined in the fun as the Stavanger man prepared to demonstrate the famous Norwegian cod kiss.

"Hold it," I said, "lemme get my camera." He held the cod as if it were a rifle, and he pointed it at himself. With great ceremony he raised the bug-eyed fish to eye level and brought it toward his face. Lips met lips, and for a moment the world stood still. When the kiss ended, we rewarded the man with applause, winces, and good-natured ribbing. He asked if I wanted to try this fish kiss, but I passed.

By now, most of the other people on board had given up fishing. One man had succumbed to seasickness and assumed the humble hunched-over-railing position so familiar to sailors and fishermen. I was getting cold, and presumably so were others. I put on my parka, then my yellow shell jacket over that. I wanted to avoid the heated cabin; the confined space would have made me seasick. We all were relieved when the guide announced we were heading back.

The Great Liquor Day

On the return trip, I offered my catch to a woman, who gratefully accepted. Cod is good eating, and all tourists want to step ashore again with fish for the freezer as well as tales for the evening. The cod kisser from Stavanger invited me to a cod dinner in Kabelvåg, a small town five kilometers south of Svolvær. Tempting, but with a few beers in him, I wasn't quite sure what he would be kissing. I was mindful of the Great Liquor Day in the Lofotens.

This tradition goes back to the end of the last century. Lofoten residents apparently were concerned about excessive drinking during the fishing season. Imagine thousands of drunken fishermen who, to keep other boats from drifting onto their claim, would resort to wielding knives, oars, and long poles with boat hooks at the end. The Great Liquor Day was an appeal to the men to save their drinking for March 25, when everyone braced for 24 hours of merriment and mayhem. Often on this day a boat owner would present his crew with a bottle of brandy, which loosened the tongue. On the Great Liquor Day, each person was, and still is, allowed to speak his or her mind to anyone—boss, spouse, or a store owner with prices too high—with impunity.

Taking in the view from the boat railing, I felt satisfied with the day. I had what I came for—the experience of fishing on arctic waters for the fish that eventually becomes lutefisk. About halfway back to shore, I realized I was in for a bonus. The clouds lifted dramatically, and the midday sun came on like a radiant hostess who knows her party is going to be a smash. The water turned from black to blue, and the mountains showed their rugged shoulders. The absolute whiteness of the mountains might have bleached out the blues of the sky and the sea, but all colors held fast. We squinted and smiled at the brilliance, then scrambled for our sunglasses and cameras.

Stocking Up on Stockfish

Asbjørn Gabrielsen grew up on the Lofotens with the hope and expectation of becoming a fisherman. Seasickness stopped him. So he uses his knowledge of the islands and fishing to help others understand and appreciate the beauty of the Lofotens. He assists tourists in his position of product coordinator at Destination Lofoten in Svolvær.

The day after my cod conquest, Asbjørn and I drove to Henningsvær, a fishing village of 600, located 26 kilometers south of Svolvær. The late afternoon drive gave us expansive views of the golden ocean when the road curved left, startling blue-white mountainscapes as the road curled right.

A bridge took us into Henningsvær, which is sometimes called "the Venice of Lofoten" because of the many buildings right on the waterways. On the main channel, fishing boats were chugging in with their catch. A cluster of tourists stood outside the open sliding door of a long, white, garage-like building, one of about 80 small, family-owned fish-processing plants on the islands. Each plant employs from two to 100 people to process the fresh fish into various products for export.

We parked and joined the crowd, which was watching a worker calf-deep in cod on the deck of a 50-foot fishing boat docked next to the plant. He was picking up fish one by one and pitching them into a big bucket. When the bucket was full, he pulled a lever, and a hoist groaned as it raised the bucket of fish. He pulled another lever to dump the catch into a gray plastic bin on the dock. The huge brown-green cod splatted heavily on top of each other. They seemed alive (but weren't) as they slurped and slithered in each other's clotty slime.

Two middle-aged men wearing rubber boots, gloves, bright orange and red chest aprons, and that it-ain't-nothin' swagger of men who clean fish in front of a crowd, worked at a table half inside, half outside the dank building. In the fading light, under a lone light bulb strung over the table, they kept a steady pace, snatching a fish by the tail and slamming it onto the gleaming aluminum tabletop strewn with blood and guts. Temperatures in the 30s seemed ideal to keep the odor down and the men from sweating.

Zip, zip, just like that they cut off the head and cleaned

the gut. They scraped the pink roe, which would become caviar, into white plastic bins and tossed the head into a bucket, chatting with each other all the while. A boy speared each fish head and cut out the tongue. He tried not to beam at the attention he received for being so young and so nifty with a knife. The men slid the gutted, headless fish down the table to sorters. The sorters sent some fish to a back room for salting and stacking cross-row on pallets, Asbjørn told me. Most of the fish they matched two by two, according to length and weight, tied the tails together, and tossed them into yet another plastic bin.

"What happens with these?" I asked Asbjørn as I pointed to the tail-tied fish.

"Come. I will show you."

We took a short drive to another, higher section of Henningsvær's craggy shoreline. There 10-foot-high wood racks held rows and rows of horizontal, 6-inch round wooden poles. Asbjørn and I watched as men draped the tail-tied cod over the poles, as if they were hanging clothes on the line to dry. We stomped through shin-high snow to get a closer look. Red speckles melted into the snow beneath the fresh fish. Asbjørn explained that the fish had to have their backs to the prevailing easterly winds to keep rain from blowing into the gutted belly and rotting it.

These flat drying racks, as well as 30-foot tall A-frame racks, surround all the fishing villages on the islands. As the season progresses, the racks fill with stockfish and the weather warms, creating quite an aroma. But fishing families don't mind—to them it is the smell of money.

"So, what is drying now will be lutefisk next Christmas?" I asked.

That used to be the case, Asbjørn explained. The top-grade fish went to the Italians, and some of the lower grade fish went to the United States, where it was soaked in water and lye to form lutefisk. However, in the 1980s U.S. lutefisk makers began the switch from cod to ling. Because it is kiln-dried, ling varies less in quality than does the cod dried outside, say lutefisk processors. Also, the backbone is removed in ling—but not Lofoten cod—before drying. This speeds the drying (less fish to dry). It also speeds the soaking by lutefisk processors and means less labor because processors do not have to remove backbones.

The trade-off, say lutefisk experts, is that ling lutefisk has less flavor. Ling is caught by Norwegian fishermen out in the open sea—often north of Scotland—on long lines. Because long lines are checked less frequently than nets, ling is often not as fresh as cod when it is brought ashore for processing, says Rolf Jentoft. Ling is kiln-dried in a few days at plants in western Norway, which, according to Jentolf, allows little time for natural seasoning. Removing the backbone for American customers—"They go crazy if they find a bone in their fish," says Jentoft—removes an element that adds flavor. The backbone, he insists, makes the cod lutefisk better than the ling.

After spending 30 minutes meandering among the drying fish, we climbed into my car, grateful to be out of the damp wind, and headed back to Svolvær. When we stopped for dinner, we ordered fresh cod (I passed on lutefisk). Over dinner, Asbjørn fretted that with serious talk of the union of European nations, too many fishing boats would make the Lofotens waters as fished out as the waters of Newfoundland. To protect the Lofoten fisheries, he hoped Norway would vote against joining the European Union. (A year later, Norway voted against joining.)

After dinner I drove Asbjørn home, then returned to my hotel. Tomorrow, Sunday, I would fly from Svolvær to Bodø to Oslo, the first legs of my trip home.

*   *   *

Flying out as I had come, amid snow, I watched the islands and mountains and fishing boats get smaller and then disappear as we rose into the snow clouds. In spite of the allure of the light and the landscape of the Lofotens, the strongest lasting image I took with me was that of the racks of fish. So fleshy and beautiful and barbaric—blood dripping, heads hacked off, covered with nets to prevent seabirds from soiling and eating the catch. The fish would dry and eventually end up on a long table in some church basement or on fine holiday china on Christmas Eve.

When I see lutefisk again back home, I thought, I will see it as something at the end of a long journey. An ending is so much more rewarding when you remember the beginning, and I knew a lutefisk dinner would never again be the same.

3

A Lazarus Act

Transforming ling into lutefisk is a bit miraculous.

Mike Field gave a good shove to the sliding back door of his enclosed truck. The door rolled up easily, exposing file cabinet–size cardboard boxes of dried stockfish, stacked floor to ceiling.

It was early November—the height of the lutefisk season. The truck was in back of Mike's Fish & Seafood, which perched on a glacial hill overlooking Glenwood, a town of 2,800 on the shores of Lake Minnewaska in west-central Minnesota. Glenwood is about two and one-half hours northwest of the Twin Cities and a stone's throw from Starbuck, where the World's Largest Lefse—9 feet, 8 inches across—was made in 1983.

Holding a pipe in his teeth, Mike picked up a 100-pound box, lowered it onto the gravel drive, and opened it. Inside, scores of brown stockfish, each weighing a pound or two and each about 2 feet long and 5 inches wide, lay like mummified body limbs. The cold outside air kept down the fishy smell.

I tried to dent the stockfish with my fingernail. Hard as a board. This light fish "stick" once resembled the 9-pound

Dried fish.
Mike Field by a 100-
pound bale of ling
stockfish from Norway.
Mike makes these dried
fish into lutefisk, which
he sells at his plant
in Glenwood, Minn.

cod I had seen caught and hung out to dry in the Lofoten Islands in Norway. Now, here at Mike's, I was about to see how this cadaverous dried fish would spring back to life, reconstituted into lutefisk.

Over the next few months, I would receive further education in the transformation of stockfish from two of the best: Bill Andresen and Obert Anderson of the Olsen Fish Co., the largest lutefisk processor in the world. Olsen Fish in north Minneapolis had been preparing lutefisk since 1910, and Bill had served as company president since 1977. A tall, well-dressed man in his 50s, Bill spoke passionately about his product.

Obert, 93 and retired, joined Olsen Fish Co. in 1923 as a bookkeeper, fresh from Minot, N.D. The company then occupied its original location: the basement of a grocery store on Seven Corners (Cedar and Riverside area). That neighborhood was also known at that time as "Snoose Boulevard," the center of the Scandinavian community. We talked in Obert's Minneapolis apartment, where he served eggnog and showed photo albums of the days when "just about" every street corner in Minneapolis had a lutefisk soaker.

Here is what I learned from Mike, Bill, and Obert about the lutefisk business.

More Ling, Less Labor

Until the early 1980s, U.S. lutefisk processors bought cod stockfish. Nowadays, the stockfish is almost always dried ling, a fish much like cod but less expensive and in some ways more appealing to consumers.

"Ling cures out whiter," said Bill Andresen, "and people eat with their eyes. The true cod, people didn't like that because it has a slightly amber color.

"Also, the ling is a little more forgiving for the cook; it doesn't cook away on you so fast. You know, you get these horror stories of, 'My God, I had all the aunts and uncles sitting there, and the lutefisk turned to mush from overcooking.' Ling won't do that so quickly.

"So the whole American market in the last 15 years has turned over to ling. Ling is very bland—you'll get more of a taste from true cod—so you really need the cream sauce or the mustard sauce or the butter to dress it up a bit. But ling turns out to be a good white product, and it has some taste to it."

Lutefisk makers prefer ling not only because it is less expensive than cod, but also because the quality of this kiln-dried fish is more consistent than the quality of air-dried cod. In 1968 when Mike first started in the lutefisk business in Brooten, Minn., the stockfish quality varied greatly, he said. Some fish dried outdoors in northern

Norway had frozen, and some from southern Norway had hung out in the rain too long. Sometimes birds pecked holes in the meat or left droppings on the dried fish.

A final reason for the switch: Ling requires less handling. Norwegian fish processors ship the dried cod with bones, a boon to flavor, they say. However, ling processors filet the fish before drying and shipping it. The boned fish takes less time to dry and soak.

"Ling is a better, cleaner product, and we get a trimmed filet," said Bill. "The neck collar is gone, the backbone's gone, the side bones are gone. All we have to do is soak it. And now there is a demand for skinless fish, which takes up 15 percent of our production. Churches like that it is ready for the pot. All they have to do is chunk it and boil it, and, my goodness, there is no more than 3 to 4 percent waste."

Lowdown on Lutefisk

Lutefisk processors use a centuries-old procedure to turn stockfish into lutefisk. Each processor adds his own special touches, but they all soak the hardened fish in water, then in a lye solution, then in water again. Lye breaks down the desiccated cell walls of the stockfish, and water causes the meat to swell up and take on a gel-like consistency. After the swelling, lutefisk processors thoroughly soak and rinse the fish in water. Then they package it for sale to customers who boil or bake it.

Those are the basics. Over lunch in the office of his Glenwood plant, Mike filled me in on some of the details of the lutefisk trade. Sitting underneath a sign that said "When lutefisk is outlawed, only outlaws will have lutefisk," we ate tuna on toast and Mike's own brand of pickled herring. After the meal, Mike puffed his pipe, and I won-

Lutefisk Jerky

Bill Andresen, president of Olsen Fish Co. in Minneapolis, recalled the days when people would peel off strips of stockfish and eat them like beef jerky.

"I once was in Norway walking through the racks of dried cod. The guy with me reached up and snapped off a hunk of fish: 'Here, try that.' Well, I've never done this before, I thought. It had a fishy taste, but a very clean taste. No bad odor. Chewy. You have to understand that dried cod was to the Vikings what pemmican was to the American Indians."

Actually, Bill had heard about this Norwegian treat years earlier. He grew up in Superior, Wis., in the 1930s when the packet steamers ran on the Great Lakes. "My dad used to tell how some of those Norwegians, while on breaks from unloading stockfish from packet freighters, used to reach in their pockets for a piece of stockfish they'd snapped off. They'd take that piece and put it in their coffee before eating it."

Five-Year-Old Fish

My wife, Jane, and I have been guests for lutefisk at the home of Odd and Randi Unstad. They live in the Twin Cities, but Odd grew up on the Lofoten Islands in Norway. He visits the Lofotens yearly, and some years he returns bearing cod stockfish. He wraps the dried fish in plastic bags, which he packs into a suitcase and checks as luggage. Back in the Twin Cities, Odd processes his own lutefisk for dinner parties that he and Randi throw each winter.

At one such party, Odd happened to mention that the lutefisk we were eating was processed and prepared from stockfish dried five years earlier and stored in his basement. Now, understand that Jane was, shall we say, a pretty pokey pilgrim in the lutefisk crusades. She sat at the table, prodding her lutefisk and ruminating on the fine line between rotting and preserving—and on the harsh measures undertaken to return this fish to edible form. Like a record needle stuck in a groove, she remarked to one dinner guest after another: "I can't believe it. I can't believe it. I'm eating 5-year-old fish!"

Norway's Lofoten Islands are 100 miles north of the Arctic Circle. For centuries this mountainous wall of 80 weather-moody islands have been famous for bounteous cod fishing and rugged beauty. This is where the story of lutefisk begins.

Overleaf: *March in Svolvær, the central city of the Lofotens. During the cod fishing season, which begins in January and ends in April, teeming shoals of cod sweep down from the Barents Sea to spawn in the Lofoten's plankton-rich waters.*

About 3,000 fishermen work the Lofoten waters in boats like this 50-footer. Half the fishermen reside on the islands; the rest come from all parts of Norway and sleep on board their modern vessels. They work six days a week and about 320 days a year.

The author catches a cod. Now, where is the lye to make lutefisk? Most cod are about 9 pounds, and a few reach 100 pounds. This fish was caught at a depth of 100 yards. The air temperature was just above freezing.

Netting used to catch cod. Fishing crews lower weighted nets 50 to 180 yards and then buoy the nets to keep them at a chosen depth. Later the same day, crews haul in the nets, which are 3 to 4 yards wide and 30 to 35 yards long.

Right: *Henningsvær, one of many fishing villages on the islands, is sometimes called "the Venice of Lofoten." Several buildings— including fish processing plants—are right on the waterways. In the afternoons, fishing boats chug in with their catch.*

Left, top: *A fisherman unloading cod. The government allows each boat a yearly quota, set according to boat length. A standard 50-foot boat has a quota of 150 tons of whole fish a year. A good day may mean a catch of 10 tons.*

Left, bottom: *Men clean the cod and remove the heads. Other workers cut out the tongues, a delicacy, and save the roe for caviar. The cleaned fish are matched two by two and tied together by the tails. The tail-tied cod hang outside on wooden drying racks.*

Tail-tied cod are draped from drying racks throughout the islands. The dried fish, called stockfish, have lost water weight and almost none of the nutritional value. Lofoten weather is ideal for drying: not too cold, which would freeze the fish, and not too hot, which would make them rot.

dered whether he smoked for pleasure or to ward off the lutefisk odor in the air. That fish smell would linger for months in the leather collar of my jacket.

Mike said each year he processes up to 50,000 pounds of stockfish, which makes 350,000 to 400,000 pounds of lutefisk. The rule of thumb is that 1 pound of stockfish swells up to 7 to 8 pounds of lutefisk.

Mike orders stockfish from Norwegian exporters, who ship ling to the East Coast. Trains carry the fish to Minneapolis. In August and again in November, he trucks stockfish from Minneapolis to Glenwood.

Mike unloads the bales of dried ling and soaks the stockfish for three or four days in livestock tanks full of water. During the company's busiest time, from August through February, Mike has eight employees. He said there can be such a rush that full tanks need to be stacked three high.

After the first soaking, the workers drain the water and refill the tanks with a lye-water solution. They stir the fish twice daily, keeping them in the lye solution for eight to 10 days, depending on the fish size. Mike said he goes through about 2½ tons of lye each soaking season.

"Lye makes the texture of the fish," he said as he led me through high-ceilinged rooms roughly the size of a small auto repair shop. Our first stop was at a 20-foot-long, thigh-high tank filled with fish filets and a white, frothy mixture of lye and water.

"You keep the fish in the lye too long, it gets mushy; too short and it is too hard," Mike said. "Even now, after all these years, I still go through and feel all my fish and make sure they're the right texture. I use what I call a thumb test. When my thumb feels right in the fish, that's when I drain the lye off."

"That's very scientific," I joked.

"Well, very scientific, you betcha," he said, playing along

Stirring lutefisk.
Mike turns fish soaking in frothy tanks of lye water.

by holding up his prized poker. "It all has to do with that thumb, which I have stuck in more fish than I care to think about."

I watched Mike demonstrate the thumb test, then tried the test myself. I grabbed a filet from the filmy lye solution and pressed my thumb into the meat. The meat had *boing*—a tough, rubbery springiness. Not quite ready, said Mike. The meat should not be that resistant. It needed another day. I quickly washed the soapy lye off my hands and wondered how Mike's hide could hold up under such repeated caustic exposures.

When the fish passes the thumb test, Mike drains the lye water. He then immerses the fish in a mixture of fresh water and hydrogen peroxide. He keeps the fish in this solution for five days, stirring twice daily. Hydrogen peroxide, he said, is not necessary; it whitens the fish for cosmetic purposes. "When we started soaking, we didn't use hydrogen peroxide. But people have gotten more particular in what they eat. It's gotta be nice and white and flaky—nice firm fish."

As we stood over a tank of fish soaking in hydrogen peroxide and water, I asked Mike if the chemicals in lutefisk bothered him. He assured me the hydrogen peroxide loses its potency and naturally degrades after three days in water, "so it is all out of the product. The lye, I imagine you never get all of that out completely. But that's where you get your flavor."

The tour ended at several tanks filled with fish soaking in plain water. After the whitening stage, Mike drains the hydrogen peroxide solution. Then he soaks the fish in fresh water for five days total, changing the water daily and stirring the fish twice daily. At this point, the lutefisk is ready for sale.

Grateful, Demanding Customers

After the soaking comes the selling. Selling lutefisk has always been a demanding business, full of frantic seasonal pushes to meet the high expectations of lutefisk loyalists. These people will glorify you when the fish is good, and gore you when it is not.

"Our audience is the most discriminating in the world," said Bill. "Why? They are old Scandinavians. You better have your ducks all in a row when you sell to these people because they know what they are buying and eating. They grew up with it in the days when their fathers prepared it at home. For example, remember the days when the toilet tanks were up on the ceiling? I had a guy tell me: 'Oh, yeah, my dad used to put the dried fish up there because he knew the water was going to be changed frequently enough.'

"Lutefisk is a touchstone. To Scandinavians it's a reminder of the best of times and the worst of times. Some-

Why Lye?

Soak fish in lye? Why? Who would do such a thing? These are questions people ask when they step back long enough from the feeding frenzy at lutefisk dinners to inquire about lutefisk's origins.

No one really knows when and how the lutefisk tradition began, says Astri Riddervold in her book Lutefisk, Rakefisk and Herring in Norwegian Tradition. *Documents from the 1500s indicate that eating lutefisk at religious festivals was a well-established tradition even then. Perhaps lutefisk began, she writes, from the practice of adding ash (for flavor) and lime (for blanching) to water used to boil dried fish. Immersing fish in ash water is almost the same as bathing them in lye, because the traditional way of preparing lye was to boil hardwood ashes in water.*

When Scandinavians are stumped about how some things get started, they have an easy out: They blame the Vikings. Minneapolis lutefisk gourmet, Odd Unstad, said legend has it that lutefisk began when plundering Vikings burned down a fishing village, including the wooden racks of drying cod. Water was poured on the racks to put out the fires. Ashes covered the dried fish, and then it rained. The fish buried in ashes thus became soaked in a lye slush. Days later villagers poking in the ashes were stunned to see the dried fish had changed to what looked like fresh fish. They rinsed the fish in the brook, and boiled it. A brave villager—or someone who drew the short straw—tasted the fish. Ummmm. Not bad.

And the rest, as they say, is history.

times it is portrayed as poor food, other times as a fun food. But it is the food that touches it all, that reminds us, that takes us home. You had the immigrants that came over—they were eating lutefisk. Then you had that first generation eating lutefisk, and then everyone after that.

"When you eat lutefisk, there's a click in the head—all those fond memories of Christmas and the talking around the table, and the friends coming in, and so on. That's why it's so disappointing if they overcook it and bring out that plate of 'glue.'

"We get a couple of letters a year from disappointed people who say, 'I served your fish and it was glue, and you guys should be shot at sunrise.'"

Scandinavians take their lutefisk seriously. Yes, they laugh at lutefisk and therefore themselves, but do not try keeping them from their dinners of choice.

"I don't know of any other ethnic food that people will stand in line for, sometimes for up to two hours," said Mike. "It isn't that everybody enjoys the lutefisk, but they'll go to a lutefisk feed because there is fellowship involved."

"You get lutefisk gypsies," quipped Bill, "who call me up and want to know where are all the lutefisk suppers this year. They go from church to church to church every weekend. To these people, eating the fish each year is almost sacred."

Those Were the Days

The lutefisk business is demanding not only because consumers have high expectations, but also because competition has been keen. Obert could tick off eight companies in Minnesota that made lutefisk in the 1930s. "There was Olsen Fish Co. and Lyon Fish Co., both of them on the same street. Kildahl Fish Co. and Ranhime Fish Co. were both in Minneapolis, and Boak Fish Co. was in St. Paul.

The lutefisk rush.
During the pre-Christmas season,
Olsen Fish Co. stacks tanks full of soaking stockfish.
This 1950s photo illustrates today's operation as well.

Duluth had Kemp Fish Co. and Hanson Fish Co., which made lutefisk for Rust Parker Grocery Co. And Bergseth Fish Co. had plants in Minneapolis, Fargo, and Minot."

Those were boom years for lutefisk, up through the 1950s. Obert said that Olsen Fish Co. alone soaked 1,000 bundles (100,000 pounds) of stockfish in a typical year. "Lutefisk was a very important part of our business, which also included herring, smoked fish, and other kinds of fish. We had good sales, profitable sales. You could buy a bundle of stockfish for around $50 [versus $1,000 today, $1,500 skinless]. You got to remember that 1 pound of stockfish became 7 or 8 pounds of lutefisk. At first, in the '30s, we sold lutefisk for 10 cents per pound [versus $2 to $2.50 today; $3 to $4 at grocery stores]."

As a comparison, Bill said each year Olsen now soaks "a

Olsen Fish Co., June 23, 1926.
*Obert Anderson, sitting cross-legged in the middle, joined the
company in 1923 as a bookkeeper from Minot, N.D. He admits
he never liked lutefisk, which sold back then for about 10 cents
per pound. Pictured, left to right, are Ray Truax, Earl Billings,
Jarry Stone, Obert, and Carl Forsberg.*

little more than 600 bundles—about the same as we did in
1977, when I joined." However, this amount included the
business brought in with the purchase of two competitors,
Kemp and Viking (a branch of Lyon Food Products). "I am
ordering just as much fish for one company as three companies did before."

Today, there are four major lutefisk processors in the
United States, said Bill. Three are in Minnesota: Olsen,
Mike's, and Day Fish Co. in Braham, Minn. The fourth is
New Day Fisheries in Port Townsend, Wash.

Wartime Lutefisk

Obert Anderson, 93, retired from the lutefisk industry in the 1980s, before the change from cod to ling. He remembered the heyday of cod fishing in Norway. "All of a sudden there would be a deluge from up north," he said. "Nice, fresh, fat cod that would strike the Lofoten Islands first. I always said the Lofotens were God's greatest gift to Norway."

Obert also remembered when World War II interrupted the supply of cod. German submarines sealed off the coast of Norway, and U.S. lutefisk processors were forced to get by with Alaska or Nova Scotia cod. The Alaska cod was a black cod, Obert said, a variety that was too fat and oily for good lutefisk. Nova Scotia cod were salted and dried on rocks, not on racks like Lofoten cod. This made for inferior lutefisk. "It wouldn't swell up as well, wouldn't take the weight," he said. "It wasn't anything like Lofoten cod. No one can dry fish like those Norwegians."

When the war ended, demand for fish products, including lutefisk, rose. "Business opened up after the war. There had been a freeze on all this, but now everybody wanted everything. Servicemen had been eating exotic foods from the world over and now, back home, they wanted shrimp, lobster tails, everything."

Obert was not among those demanding more lutefisk. "I shouldn't admit it, but I never had any liking for lutefisk. Both mom and dad were born in Norway, and we had lutefisk for the holidays. We ate it whether we liked it or not."

Will the Lutefisk Tradition Die Out?

The practice of soaking lutefisk at home began fading out in the 1950s. People were content to let the church or the lodge make lutefisk, thus avoiding the smell and the hassle at home. Also, consumers wanted more fast food, which lutefisk is not (although one church has hawked lutefisk-on-a stick at the Minnesota State Fair).

Today, church dinners seem to be thriving; however, both the diners and the volunteers are mostly elderly. How many more years can these good people do the cooking and cleaning and serving at the dinners? "You call on churches now, and the buyers are quite elderly," said Bill. "They talk about, 'Well, I don't know, maybe this is our last year because we just lost our head of the lefse committee.' It's very tough to get people to do this kind of thing.

"I'm worried, for obvious business reasons. But also, we are going to lose all this heritage some day. There will still be strongholds, but in the next 10 years we'll see a big reduction. It hasn't fallen off as fast as some people predicted 10 to 15 years ago. They said that by the mid-'90s there would be practically nothing left, and that is not the case at all.

"We still produce more lutefisk in Minnesota—all three producers—than in all the Scandinavian countries combined. In Finland, Sweden, and Norway we see an increase in consumption, but they don't get this constant bad press as we do here in the United States. Stuff like: 'You got rats? Just stick some lutefisk under the porch and you'll get rid of them.' Or 'What's that awful smell? The garbage dump overflowing or the lutefisk factory?'"

"When I first started," said Mike, "all the stories were: 'Gee, don't get into the lutefisk business, it's dying. The old timers are dying off, and the new generation is not eating

The olden days of big cod and big catches. *Bill Andresen: "We are not seeing as many big fish anymore," he says, referring to these 1940s photos from Norway's Lofoten Islands (left). "Fishermen are always catching ahead now, meaning this year's class of fish probably should not have been harvested until the turn of the century."*

it.' Well, the tradition goes on. You're now seeing a lot of 40-year-olds at the suppers, and the 18- and 19-year-olds will develop a taste for it. Lutefisk is just something that you don't eat a whole bunch of at first. But if you keep at it ... well, it can get embarrassing at some of these dinners. I've seen guys come in and eat about 5 to 6 pounds. They paid their $7.50, and they didn't come to eat meatballs, I'll tell you that."

A few years ago, Mike introduced a TV-dinner called Michael's Classic Lutefisk Meal. Stick it in the microwave, and in a few minutes you've got hot lutefisk, mashed potatoes, and corn. It is convenient, which appeals to busy, middle-age customers who for the first time may be experiencing coming-of-age urges for lutefisk.

"The first year we introduced the TV-dinner in March," said Mike, "and at the end of May we had sold over 6,000 dinners."

All in all, said Mike, the future is bright for lutefisk. You won't ever be able to call lutefisk a growth industry; lutefisk won't leak outside the Scandinavian community. However, he said, if you give people a good product—and convenience—they will come out.

"It isn't that the crowds are less at these suppers," Mike said. "It's that the people putting them on can't do it anymore." He was of a mind that in the changing of the guard, from elderly to middle-aged volunteers at lutefisk dinners, there is, and will be, a shake-down. But the next generation will show up, he said. It is their time.

"I'll tell you this," said Mike, "in my business we've had more churches start lutefisk dinners than quit. As long as tradition is important in our lifestyle, lutefisk will continue on."

4

Big Doings at Big Canoe

In Iowa farm country, some seafood is sacred.

Part of the draw of a lutefisk church dinner is the chance to sit—duty free—in a sanctuary. Just sit. How many of us do that anymore? Just sit for a while with our thoughts, as the early evening light flows through stained-glass windows, turns amber, and falls on our shoulders. No singing. No standing, sitting, pledging, reading, fussing with kids. Perhaps lutefisk dinners have long waits because the parishioners come early just to feel the embrace of their sanctuary. Such was the case for me as I waited for my lutefisk inside the Big Canoe Lutheran Church near Decorah, Iowa.

Every year on the second Sunday in November, Big Canoe puts on one of the best lutefisk feeds you can imagine. I had left Minneapolis at 5 in the morning and driven two and one-half hours to get to the church in time to witness the preparations for the 4 o'clock dinner.

When I parked my car in the church lot, I noticed that it would not have taken much to coax snow out of the dull, gray clouds. I followed my nose to the basement kitchen. I could hear the rattly whir of electric knives—no doubt,

Big Canoe Lutheran Church, Decorah, Iowa.
Parishioners put on one fine lutefisk feed.

the workers were skinning lutefisk and chunking the filets.

Once inside, I met Marcy Amundson. I knew Marcy from my visit to Decorah to research my lefse book five years earlier. Marcy showed me a freezer full of wrapped lefse and the tabletop groaning with lefse thawing for the meal. The lefse, she explained, was the product of 24 workers who got together to make 45 dozen lefse rounds on eight griddles. (Looking down the list of lefse rollers, I saw the names of three men: Steve Emery, Mavis Arneson, and Pastor Dave Andreae. Hurrah, guys! Whenever I can, I like to support men who roll.)

Next, Marcy showed me several blue plastic containers the size of garbage cans, full of peeled potatoes covered with water to keep them from turning dark; pails of ready-to-cook rutabagas; and a large electric cooker of meatballs and gravy. She opened the fridge packed full with butter, milk, and dishes covered with aluminum foil. No doubt about it, a lot of food—enough for 600 people.

Rutabaga row.
Pails of peeled rutabagas, ready to be boiled, will be served to about 600 diners at Big Canoe.

Team Rutabaga

Big Canoe's lutefisk dinner served rutabagas grown for the meal. Don Hanson had seeded rutabagas with his oats, which he harvested long before digging up the rutabagas. I asked Don if rutabagas were a good cash crop. "No," he snorted, "they are non-profitable. No one wants to buy rutabagas."

Supper for 600

Thinking about having a lutefisk dinner at your church or lodge? You will need a few things, so check the shopping list of the Big Canoe Lutheran Church:

600 lb. lutefisk (1 lb. per person)
30 lb. salt
240 lb. potatoes
30 lb. rutabagas
14 gallons corn
170 lb. meatball mix (ground by butcher,
  who adds spices as well)
20–30 lb. soup bones (for gravy)
2 boxes Pillsbury brown gravy mix
1 case canned beef gravy
1 dozen onions
20 trays (about 350) of bakery finger rolls
60 lb. butter
8 lb. brown sugar
9 lb. drip coffee
5 cartons half & half
2 gallons milk (for cooking)
200 cartons milk (individual servings)
45 dozen lefse rounds

Shopping list for lefse making:
140 lb. potatoes
10 lb. butter or margarine
50 lb. flour
3 lb. powdered sugar
4 boxes of plastic bags
4 large rolls aluminum foil
1 double package napkins
2 lb. coffee

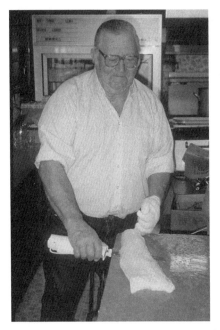

Team captain.
Don Hanson uses an electric knife to skin the fish. Don is also captain of Team Rutabaga.

Each autumn Don recruited a few good men—Team Rutabaga—to help harvest. The six-member team also showed up to help prepare 30 pounds of rutabagas for dinner. Loren Amundson washed the rutabagas; Don Hanson himself removed the rutabaga tops and tips with a band saw; Nels Gavle, Ross Arneson, and Bob Wedmann peeled; and Pastor Dave cut the rutabagas into strips.

"How did the cooks prepare the lutefisk?" I asked Marcy. The volunteers opened a dozen 50-pound, plastic-lined boxes of lutefisk and washed the fish the previous Thursday, she said. In a large kettle, they mixed 5 pounds of salt with water to make a brine. They placed the filets in layers in a large tub, pouring brine over each layer of fish. When the tub was full, they added enough water to cover the fish. The next evening the volunteer crew poured off the brine and covered the fish with water. The next day, Saturday, they changed the water. Sunday the fish were ready for skinning and cutting into 6-inch squares.

The time was now 8:45 a.m. The crew took a break for coffee and donuts. Eunice Stoen, another long-time friend, arrived. I had featured Euny in my lefse book—she once made lefse for a New York City dinner party hosted by actress Arlene Dahl—and she is author of several cookbooks. Her father, Rev. W.T. Hexom, served as pastor of Big Canoe from 1939 until his death in 1965.

Euny was in a goofy mood that Sunday morning—the promise of lutefisk can do that to people. She was wearing a sweatshirt that said: "I put the fun in dysfunctional."

"Does the sweatshirt have anything to do with your love of lutefisk?" I kidded her.

"Oh no," she said, "I don't like lutefisk."

"Is that dysfunctional—that you don't like lutefisk?"

A real pair.
Coffee with Marcy Amundson
and Eunice Stoen (in the funny sweatshirt).

"No," came the quick response, "it would be dysfunctional if I did."

Ole and Lena
and Pastor Dave

Just before church, I asked Marcy if we could go up to see the sanctuary. We climbed the stairs, and she turned on the lights. We passed through the open sanctuary doors and stood for a moment.

I had expected a box-shaped room, not such stately beauty. The lofty, curved ceiling gave an openness to an interior that otherwise might have seemed confined. Light danced on the varnished moldings, floorboards, and polished wood columns that supported a balcony over the rear quarter of the room. I peeked up at the balcony and saw a pipe organ, flanked by pews.

Two chandeliers lit the transept, the space that runs at right angles to the nave, forming the shape of a cross when viewed from above. I was surprised to see a transept in a church this small. Each wing had tall, broad, stained-glass windows and a half dozen pews, facing the open space in front of the altar.

An arch of wood molding framed the dome over the altar, which sat on a semi-circular stage rimmed with a low wood railing. Behind the altar, against the wall and ornately framed, was an elevated 5-foot-tall statue of Christ and smaller statues of Mark and Luke. A wood pulpit stood on a 3-foot-tall platform, enclosed by waist-high walls.

People were arriving early for the service, so Marcy and I took a seat. I wanted to sit toward the back so I could slip out early and see Stanley Iverson pull the rope to ring the church bells at the end of the service. Most of the congregation sat at the back of the church. In fact, so many sat in

Statues of Christ, Mark, and Luke.
At the turn of the century, the statues and altar
were sent by train from Milwaukee to nearby Calmar,
then hauled by wagon to Big Canoe.

Sanctuary order.
Pews and hymnals, as seen from Big Canoe's balcony.

the back that I wondered if the front pews had been varnished the day before (they were not).

After a few scripture readings and hymns, Pastor Dave took the pulpit and began his sermon, "Are We on Speaking Terms With God?" I liked the sermon. I admire a preacher who has courage enough to use an Ole and Lena joke to make his point. Pastor Dave's point: God wants to hear directly from each of us; we should confess our own sins, not someone else's.

Well, said Pastor Dave, it seemed that Ole and Lena were listening to an evangelist preach hellfire and brimstone. The preacher asked for those who thought they were perfect to stand up. Ole stood.

"So," said the evangelist, bearing down on Ole, "you think you are perfect."

"Well, no sir," said Ole with a shrug. "It's not me I'm standing up for. It's for Lena's first husband."

After the sermon, we sang hymn 340, *"Jesus Christ, My Sure Defense."* Next came the offering and announcements. To witness the bell-ringing, I began walking out as Pastor Dave was making an announcement about some Minneapolis man visiting that day. Odd, I thought; two of us from Minneapolis were here. Just as I left the sanctuary, I heard Pastor Dave say *my* name. He went on to say he was honored I was here observing Big Canoe's lutefisk dinner for a book I was writing.

By the time I realized what had happened, I was out the sanctuary door. I imagined smiling faces turning only to see someone slinking out the door. I could not really go back in to take a bow, all red-faced and beaming. So I decided to cut my losses and let Pastor Dave figure out something. I would apologize later. I climbed the balcony stairs to see the bell tolled.

From the balcony I heard Pastor Dave give the benedic-

Ending the worship. *Stanley Iverson rings the church bells every Sunday.*

tion. Then Stanley twice pulled the rope coming through a hole in the ceiling. I wished all churches would turn off the electronic gadgetry and let people ring their bells.

After church I went to the basement to hang out around the kitchen until lunch. Women were placing small Norwegian flags on the 20 or so tables. There was not much left to do before the first seating for dinner, so Marcy and the others were heading home. I drove to the Stoen farm. Euny had invited me for lunch.

Wilbur, Euny's husband, and their son, Bill, operate the family's 604-acre dairy and hog farm. Wilbur's family has been farming in these parts since they came over from Norway in 1850. Harald and Ole Stoen had donated an acre of land for the original Big Canoe church in 1863. You could see the present church from the Stoens' dining room window.

Norwegians Honor Big Canoe

In 1843 two Norwegian immigrants came to Fort Atkinson in northeastern Iowa to farm. By 1853 more Norwegian immigrants had arrived, and they established Big Canoe Lutheran Church, named in honor of Winnebago Chief Big Canoe. His grandmother, Glory in the Morning, married a French officer, Sabrevoir De Carrie, who resigned from the army, joined the tribe, and became a fur trader. The De Carrie name changed to Dekaury and then to Decorah, now a town 13 miles southwest of the church.

Church members held services in their homes until 1863, when volunteers began building a stone church. In 1902 they dismantled the stone church and used the rock as a foundation for the present brick church, which they built across the road. The parishioners shipped the altar and its statues from Milwaukee by train to nearby Calmar, then hauled them by wagon to Big Canoe.

In 1991 the church added a new entry and an elevator. At the same time, church members nosing around in the tower found the old kerosene chandeliers that had been retired with the advent of electricity. The chandeliers were refurbished, electrified, and reinstalled. They adorn the sanctuary today.

The Supper—at Last

When the Stoens and I walked into the church around 3:30 that afternoon, people were already waiting in the sanctuary for their fish. Even the front pews were filling. I returned to the downstairs kitchen where preparations were in full swing.

At this point no one checked the duty list on the wall because they all knew what needed to be done. Shirley Bigler was mashing potatoes, Irene Tilleros was arranging lefse on plates, Helen Stegen was setting out rolls, and Margaret Rude and Ardeth Iverson were arranging plates of bars, *krumkake* (cone cookies), and other treats.

Steve Emery, Gary Stortz, and Ross Arneson were tightening some nuts on a mechanized potato masher. In a trial run, a wobbly flywheel had flown off, putting the hurt on Steve's knee. Before long the men flipped the switch and the machine hummed beautifully. An electric motor on a

Squashing spuds. *Shirley Bigler does the potato mash.*

72

Boiling bag.
*Helen Hendrickson boils lutefisk inside cheesecloth bags,
which she stitches together.*

plank turned a fan belt that wrapped around a flywheel off
an old Allis-Chalmers combine. The flywheel turned the
handle of a meat grinder. The men popped boiled potatoes
and chunks of butter into the top of the grinder and got
mashed potatoes almost instantly. Pretty slick.

At 4 o'clock seating began. Helen Hendrickson, a tall,
trim, red-haired woman in her 50s, was already cooking
lutefisk in big, covered kettles. Into the boiling water she
dropped chunks of lutefisk enclosed in four cheesecloth
bags, which Helen had made herself. "That was like
sewing on feathers, stitching together that cheesecloth,"
she told me with a chuckle. Use pickling salt in the water,
Helen advised, because coarse salt makes the lutefisk
flakier. The lutefisk would be ready in about 10 minutes,
when the fish started to "flake out. But don't boil the fish
until it falls apart," Helen cautioned me. "As a cook, you
don't want to serve that in public."

Ingenious contraption. Steve Emery puts boiled potatoes in the homemade mechanized potato masher. An electric motor turns a flywheel off an old Allis-Chalmers combine.

Helen said she and other volunteers liked working the dinner and being an active part of the community. The lutefisk brings back memories, she said, "and we all still feel wanted and needed. It unites us into a task."

As she spoke I could see a growing concern on her face. The gas stove was being stingy with the heat, making it tough to boil the fish and potatoes fast enough to keep up with demand. After a brief huddle with others stationed at the stove, someone called in Stanley Iverson, the handyman and bellringer. He hooked up a new tank of propane, and soon blue flames powered high heat from the burners.

I looked around the kitchen and noticed two dish washers up to their elbows in suds. I walked over to the sink and met Margaret Arneson and Linda Wedmann. "So, they gave you the glamour jobs," I said with a smile.

"Oh, yeah. This is it," Margaret chuckled. She nodded at the two men across the sink and said, "This must be glamour because you don't get them to dry at home."

Ralph and Stanley Arneson responded with slight smiles and innocent "who-me" looks. Then they started drying, lips pursed, white towels circling on white dishes. Why wasn't an automatic dishwasher used, I wondered. I answered my own question: Why bother? Volunteers can do dishes faster and have more fun.

Well, I had had enough talking about lutefisk. I was hungry. I headed upstairs to the sanctuary, where I waited with the rest of the crowd. And there I sat, grateful for a moment of doing nothing.

Before long, a voice called me from my pre-lutefisk meditation. My number was up, so I followed my group downstairs to the dining room and promptly took a seat. Children from the congregation were serving and clearing dishes from the tables. The lutefisk came immediately, as did a dizzying array of dishes: bowls of potatoes, gravy, meatballs, corn, and rutabagas; plates of butter, rolls, and lefse; cartons of milk; pitchers of cream; and pots of coffee. Around and around the table, we passed the food.

Sharon Anderson sat down beside me. Originally from Decorah, she came back to the Big Canoe for the lutefisk dinner. She told me the name of her new town, but I could not hear it: The noise at lutefisk dinners can be overwhelming, what with the people greeting each other, laughing at jokes, and asking for more food.

Across from me, Pam Anderson spooned lutefisk onto her plate. She paused, soberly looking at the fish. I sensed it coming. "I have a cold, and I cannot smell this lutefisk," she said with a grin. "So I guess I can eat it."

5

Confessions of a Lutefisk Gypsy

Lutefisk led to my lost weekend in Seattle.

I had been eating a lot of lutefisk—and liking it. Every weekend I attended another lutefisk dinner. Same fine fish, different friendly faces. So many dinners, so little time.

My friends were starting to worry, especially when I told them of plans to travel to the Seattle-Tacoma area for three lutefisk dinners in three nights. One friend, Michael Murphy, expressed shock at how far I had slipped. He knew me from my detest-lutefisk days and suspected I was approaching toxic levels of lutefisk. "Stop!" he shouted over the phone, perhaps imagining the red-alert sirens blaring in my lye-loaded liver. "Spare me the gory details."

I assured Mike that this was all in the name of research for my book. But whom was I kidding? Lutefisk had a hold on me, and it was taking me to Seattle.

My morning flight passed over magnificent Mount Rainier. I had visited Seattle in the 1980s to climb that 14,410-foot mountain. I pushed my limits then, and I was pushing my limits now with these three lutefisk dinners.

I picked up my rental car and headed north. Ferries and boats were crossing the bay. On this sunny, mild late-October day, the water, tall pines, and hills reminded me of

Oslo, Norway. I had a few hours before my first dinner, so I decided to visit Alf Lunder Knudsen, Ph.D., editor and publisher of the *Western Viking*, a Norwegian-American weekly newspaper.

I headed west off Interstate 5 toward Ballard, Seattle's Scandinavian community. Because King Harald V and Queen Sonja of Norway had visited Ballard the day before, Norwegian flags hung everywhere along Market Street. I parked my car and entered the small, comfy second-floor office of the *Western Viking*.

I introduced myself to Dr. Knudsen, a native Norwegian with a long beard and kind, clear blue eyes. We chatted about his big day with the King and Queen. In recognition of his 40 years of leadership in Seattle's Norwegian community and his recent award of Knight of the Royal Norwegian Order of Merit, he had been chosen to walk at the side of the royal couple in the Ballard parade.

The conversation turned to me and my lutefisk book. He asked what I did when not writing books about lutefisk and lefse. I told him I wrote magazine articles about health and fitness. His eyes twinkled, then he asked with a straight face: "Can you be into health and fitness and still eat lutefisk?" I paused, not knowing how to read him. Then he laughed when I responded that one leads to the other—eating lutefisk drives you toward a compensatory healthy lifestyle.

I asked what he thought of the humor linked to lutefisk. He said that the "humor comes up short, usually."

Administrative assistant Julie Schmidt stopped typing and pointed out upcoming lutefisk dinners listed in that week's paper. Under the headline "CALL TO LUTEFISK," I read this definition: "Lu·te·fisk \lū-tĕ·fisk\ n. 1: preserved codfish, 2: a delicacy to Norwegians, 3: a mystery to non-Norwegians. (Vesterdalen Lodge 2–131)"

Lutefisk Gig in Gig Harbor

After lunch I drove south to Tacoma, where I met Audun Toven, an associate professor and chair of the Scandinavian area studies program at Pacific Lutheran University in Tacoma. Together, we were going to Gig Harbor for a big feed at the Peninsula Lutheran Church.

We drove to Gig Harbor, a town of about 2,000 people. The Friday rush hour made for slow going as we crossed the Narrows Bridge. At the Gig Harbor exit, a painted figure of a woman in her *bunad* pointed the way to the lutefisk dinner. Another painted figure, a Viking man, pointed out a second turn. One more figure marked the entrance to the church's jammed parking lot.

At the church we were diverted by a familiar smell coming from a nearby shed. We walked to the shed and entered a steamy room, lit by two bare light bulbs. There we met

Any connection?
Directions to the lutefisk dinner at Peninsula Lutheran Church.

Bob Nelson, who was boiling the fish, and his father-in-law, Wayne Greer. Wayne crowed that he was "the only Georgia boy who ever cooked and loved lutefisk." I believed him.

Johnny Johnson, who was cutting fish, lit up when I told him I came from Minneapolis. He was born in Fergus Falls, Minn., and lived part of his childhood near Duluth. "Cold? The coldest winter I ever spent was the 4th of July in Duluth," he chuckled. (Mark Twain said something similar about San Francisco.)

We left the cook shed and purchased our tickets in the entryway to the filled sanctuary. During the next half hour, Audun introduced me to so many people that I could not remember their names. He always mentioned I had traveled all the way from Minneapolis to eat lutefisk and do research for a new book. One woman asked to which Lu-

Cooks for the big feed.
Bob Nelson, Wayne Greer, and Johnny Johnson, (left to right)
prepare fish for Peninsula Lutheran. Wayne calls himself
"the only Georgia boy who ever cooked and loved lutefisk."

theran congregation I belonged. I confessed that I was not Lutheran. Before I could add that I had been raised Lutheran, she dismissed me with a friendly, "Oh, what do you know."

A moment later a man said Minnesota was "the Holy Land. Lots of Lutherans back there." Another man said, with respect, that Minnesota was "the old country." Finally, an elderly woman, after hearing I was from Minneapolis said, "Don't you get enough lutefisk back there?"

Pastor Russell Hillman approached and introduced himself. He told me this was his first year at Peninsula Lutheran, after spending years preaching in Montana. He said the church would serve 1,400 people the next two nights—but he would not be one of them. "I tasted lutefisk once," he said, shaking his head. "That was once too often."

Not a loyalist. *Pastor Russell Hillman's congregation valued his courage when he admitted in a sermon he did not like lutefisk.*

I asked him about the neon green "Legalize Lutefisk!" sign on his office wall. He said it was a gift, perhaps out of sympathy, from the congregation. He had mentioned in his sermon the previous Sunday that he could not stand lutefisk. Based on comments he had heard since, he judged that the congregation valued his courage for confessing his shortcomings before the flock. "Others have since confided in me that they, too, don't like lutefisk," he said.

Pastor Hillman evidently had a sense of humor—which is sometimes lacking in Lutherans before a lutefisk feed. For example, he told me about an encounter he had had that afternoon: With a sad face he had greeted a carload of people who arrived for an early seating. "I approached them and said, 'I hate to tell you this, folks, but we've had to cancel the lutefisk dinner. There's a McDonald's down the road.' I then told them I was just joking, but I couldn't even get them to smile."

When Audun and I were called to eat, I thanked Pastor Hillman and shook his hand (half wondering if he was palming a buzzer). We entered the dining hall, which had about 20 round tables. Women in *bunads* served us immediately. We passed bowls and filled our plates. I had run out of room on my plate when the meatballs came around. I shrugged and piled them on my potatoes. One meatball rolled onto the lutefisk, which did not bother me. "You mix your meatballs with your lutefisk?" said Audun, eyebrows raised. "It must be the way you do it in the Midwest."

After a long flight and a big build-up to the dinner, I was famished. I savored the lutefisk, lefse, and potatoes while listening to Audun tell his mumps-and-lutefisk story. A native Norwegian, he came down with the mumps after he had moved to Seattle. He was staying in a boarding house, he said, and the owner "thought lutefisk was such a soothing food for a sick Norwegian." I could just see the bumper sticker: Dump the Mumps With Lutefisk.

After dinner I spent an hour chatting with some of the volunteers. At a table near the dining hall entrance, Joyce Sears and Mary Ross sat folding lefse and placing the

rounds on plates. Mary wore a *bunad* hand-stitched by relatives in Norway during World War II. She said her name was changed from Rorstad when in 1926, at age 4, she came over from Norway. She remembered being fed oranges on the boat during the passage. Her family settled five miles south of Gig Harbor, living on the water, catching cod right outside their door. "My mother and father used to make lutefisk in our basement," she recalled. "We had to daily change the water they used to soak the fish."

A month before the dinner, Joyce, Mary, and about 20 other women had made lefse for the dinner. "Preparing for this dinner and working here now bring back the tradition of hard work and loyalty to the community," said Joyce, her fingers in constant motion as she folded lefse.

"We work like the dickens from 12:30 to 8:00, but we have so much fun," added Mary.

"People don't necessarily eat lutefisk for the taste," continued Joyce. "They eat it as a rite of passage each year, a tradition to pass on to their children. It's a reminder of the courage it took to come to America."

After sampling a round or two of lefse—purely for quality-control purposes—I talked with people waiting tables. Anita Shomshak, a woman in her 40s, said she enjoyed talking with the older people who come in "a party mood, ready for an ethnic adventure." Ghita Lorenz, a native German, pointed out that the two months of preparing for the meal helped people make friends and helped the church attract new members.

I commented to Karen and Mike Cameron, co-chairs of the event, that it was nice to see teens and middle-aged volunteers. At many church dinners all the volunteers are elderly. "We make it a point for this to be an intergenerational thing," said Karen. "The kids can't wait each year to help out."

On my way out, I spotted Kathy Ueland across the room. She was carrying her 3-month-old daughter, Rachel, on her shoulder and waving a small Norwegian flag to signal the ticket takers that a table was ready for more customers. "I'm breaking her in early," said Kathy of her baby. "She likes the smell of lutefisk—I think."

***Baby's first
lutefisk bash.***
*Kathy Ueland
holds 3-month-old
daughter, Rachel,
while seating
lutefisk customers.*

Play Day Around Poulsbo

At 7 the next morning, a gray, still Saturday, I drove north
on the Kitsap Peninsula, across Puget Sound from Seattle,
to the famed "Little Norway" town of Poulsbo (pop. 5,000).
Gus Bjorlee, whom I was meeting for breakfast, was going
to be my tour guide.

When I arrived at the house Gus built in Silverdale, six
miles from Poulsbo, he invited me in and asked, "Do you
want a little coffee and nothing?" It was his way of saying
coffee was all he could offer at the moment.

"Yes, thanks," I said, "and I'll take two orders of
nothing."

Gus was the long-time cook at Bremerton's big lutefisk
feed, hosted by his Sons of Norway lodge, Oslo 35. He said

when his parents came from Norway in 1896, the Silverdale area was thick with Norwegians and Swedes, who had come for the lumber, fishing, farming, and gold.

Gus was born in 1918. He remembered helping his mother, Thora, make lutefisk. "Stores got their fish from the Bering Sea. A sailboat came into Poulsbo with the dried fish, you know, salted down at the time. You've probably heard the stories about grocers putting dried fish out on the sidewalks where the dogs could get to it, made it taste better. I can tell you I saw it out on the sidewalk, but not where any dog could get to it. The dried fish was out there in boxes. Or the fish would be in big crocks, soaking, right there at the grocery store in Poulsbo.

"My mother would get the dry stuff, see, possibly 3 feet long, dry like a board. I used to saw it for her with a carpenter's saw into, say, 6- to 8-inch chunks. Then she'd mix up the lye and the water in a big 20-gallon stone crock. For about two weeks that crock had to be emptied every day and filled with clean water. That was a steady job, you know.

"We even used to feed the church, a small church. We fed, oh, I don't know, 100 people maybe. The neighbor lady, Mrs. Storvik, used to come up and help. They used to put on a little feed and charge some money just for the church. Of course, your silverware turned black after a while and really had to be scrubbed up to get clean again."

Gus said the fish nowadays still comes from Canada and the Bering Sea near Alaska, but it is smaller. He said fish companies brag that they sell no fish under 33 inches. "Well, it used to be all our fish never even got close to that small," he scoffed. "The bigger the fish, the easier it is to cook. It won't turn to mush so quick."

It was a little past 9 a.m. when Gus's wife, Minnie, a late riser, joined us in the kitchen. I saw through the window that the sun was starting to burn off the clouds. The conversation turned to lutefisk's smell. "I don't think it smells as bad now as when Gus's mother was fixing it," Minnie said as she poured herself some coffee. "Oh, uff-da. I don't know what in the world it was, but it was terrible. You'd almost think you were in the wrong room."

"The wrong room?" I was not sure what she meant. Both Gus and Minnie grinned at me, then I figured it out—she meant the bathroom. Gus explained that in the old days the lutefisk processors probably did not get as much lye out of the finished product as they do now.

I asked Gus how he got roped into making lutefisk at big dinners. Sometimes it's easier to do things yourself, he explained.

Gus had been president of Oslo 35 back in 1975. The lodge had always hired cooks to prepare the fish for their dinner. That year, the cooks arrived with the fish and open whiskey bottles. They started boiling the fish but must

Little Norway tour guides.
Gus and Minnie Bjorlee parked in front of their garage.

have had the burner on low, because after a long wait no one had any lutefisk.

"I went up to them and said, 'You haven't got any fish yet.' The cooks assured me it was coming, it was coming. Well, the fish that was first served had been lying in luke-warm water, barely thawed out."

"Oh, you mean those guys from Poulsbo?" Minnie said. Gus tried to shush her from telling specifics about these cooks. "They were from Poulsbo, and they were supposed to be Norwegians."

"Okay, okay," continued Gus. "They kept serving fish, but pretty soon someone complained. So I looked at the fish. I thought: That can't be! A little ice was in the middle of it. What a mess."

The next year, the lodge cooked for themselves. Gus helped build three gas cookers, and the lodge purchased four 15-gallon stainless steel pots. The crowd was pretty thin because of the disaster the previous year, but the 300 who showed up ate "fish that turned out beautiful," said Gus. He has been cooking lutefisk ever since, for dinners that draw up to 1,200 people.

We were all getting hungry, so we drove to Poulsbo for breakfast at Henry's Restaurant. Gus and Minnie said they were buying. Looking out the window, we saw that the clouds had lifted, exposing the formidable Olympic Mountains to our west. It was turning out to be a bright, mild day.

After breakfast we toured the quaint community on the shores of Liberty Bay. Gus said that Norway's King and Queen had been up to Poulsbo a couple days before. It seemed I was destined to follow in royal footsteps.

We drove along Front Street. Scandinavian goodies beckoned from the window at Sluys Poulsbo Bakery. We continued to the marina and saw the fishing boats and seabirds. We passed by a tall white church, the First Lutheran Church of Poulsbo, which sits high on a hill and can be seen for miles around.

It was late morning and the day was getting on, so we drove back to Silverdale. Before saying good-bye, Gus showed me a lefse turning stick he had carved out of cedar. He inscribed "Gustav" into the handle of each stick before giving it away. He said he would send one to me. (He was true to his word.)

Driving back to Gig Harbor, I smiled when I recalled something Gus said about getting old: "They say old lutefisk cookers never die. They just waft away."

I drove back to Gig Harbor for another lutefisk dinner at Peninsula Lutheran Church. After the meal, I ran into Vern Peterson, a 90-something lutefisk processor of some renown. When I first talked with Vern on the telephone a few weeks earlier, he told me he did not want to talk much. Then, for the next 20 minutes, he covered lutefisk A to T, back to F, and finally to Z. It was a wild conversation, and now I enjoyed meeting him in person. Again he said he did not want to talk much. This time he meant it; lutefisk called.

Could I Stand More Lutefisk in Stanwood?

Early Sunday morning, as the sun was burning off fog and patches of clouds, I drove to Stanwood (pop. 3,000), 60 miles north of Seattle. The Lions Club there was hosting its 43rd annual lutefisk dinner at the high school, drawing up to 1,400 people, including Scandinavians from nearby British Columbia.

I entered the high school and walked into the cafeteria. I met Jim Lund, one of the honchos for the dinner. He introduced me to the workers I call the "kitchen characters."

Something about cutting up slabs of lutefisk brings out people's peculiarities, usually expressed by jokes and kidding. For example, one fish cutter at this event, Bob McCann, hit me with a day-brightener right off. "Lutefisk," he said, looking at his hands, "is the only food I know that you must wash your hands *before* you go to the bathroom." Let's just say it's a good thing these guys are in the back room while the public eats.

I decided to clear out of the kitchen and talk with the diners. Harriet Jean was eating with a friend who gave her name as Mrs. Robert Hall, originally from Starbuck, Minn. Harriet told about a lutefisk dinner she attended when she was 8-years-old. A man "who normally wandered around town dirty" sat next to her just when the lutefisk was served. Harriet moved away because she thought the man smelled. "My uncle laughed and said, 'He wasn't what you were smelling, Harriet. It was the lutefisk.'"

Mrs. Hall felt it appropriate to give me a lutefisk cheer. After all, we were dining in a high school cafeteria. "It goes like this," she said:

> Lutefisk and lefse
> *Hva skal du ha?* (What shall you have?)
> Lincoln High School
> Ya, Ya, Ya!

I moved on and heard curious information about the curative powers of lutefisk. It came from 87-year-old Ole Eide. His brother, Harry, had been battling prostate cancer. "It was to the point where we questioned if he was ready to go, if you know what I mean," said Ole. "Then someone brought him a big feed of lutefisk. From that day on, he really improved and lived three more years. He died at age 96."

Outside the cafeteria was the holding pen for folks waiting for food. I think most people would rather wait in a

Longevity testimonial.
Ole Eide, 87, tells about the curative powers of lutefisk.

serene sanctuary than a hall outside a cafeteria. But Harry Linbeck did his best to entertain the ticket holders.

Harry was the warm-up act for the big show, the lutefisk dinner. He told jokes and threatened to play his accordion. He had the voice of a carny barker, and he was owner of a dance hall where the likes of Lawrence Welk, Guy Lombardo, Wayne King, Louis Armstrong, and Myron Floren had played.

Harry, who walked with a cane, perched on a bar stool. "I've had four hips, four knees, and work done on my spine," he told me. He said old football injuries and arthritis have done the damage. "I'm not supposed to stand or sit, but who else is going to do this?"

I sensed he wouldn't miss this gig for the world, and a gang of burly Norskies would have to drag him out by his heels when the time came for him to retire. He could not stop yakking.

She Ran for Governor—

Waiting for her lutefisk at the 43rd annual Lions Club lutefisk dinner in Stanwood, Wash., Emma Repp, 94, wore dark sunglasses, which gave her a Garbo-look. In fact, Emma had had a career on the stage. "I've sung all the way from Mount McKinley to Casablanca," she said.

Exact dates were a little fuzzy to Emma, but she said in the 1930s she left a career in teaching (her most famous student was Sen. Henry Jackson of Washington) and went to Europe to sing. In France she auditioned for work singing Wagner. "The director said, 'You're not a mezzo soprano, you're a Wagnerian soprano,'" Emma recalled. "I said, 'I don't care what you call me if you call me for work.'"

During World War II, she did many New York City concerts for the Norwegian resistance. When the war ended, she received the St. Olav Medal from King Haakon. In the years right after the war, she appeared in two Broadway musicals, Street Scene, *and* Sleepy Hollow, *"which* The New Yorker *said was both sleepy and hollow," quipped Emma.*

In the early 1930s, Emma ran for governor on the Lutefisk Party ticket. All in fun, of course, but KJR radio asked her to make several broadcasts to her loyal constituency. She wrote a campaign speech, which she could still recite. The beginning went like this:

"Ladies and yentlemen, and anybody else that may be listening.

"I vant to introduce myself as candidate for governor on the Lutefisk Party ticket. I feel very vell qualifications for the yob. I granulated at the foot of my class with

on the Lutefisk Ticket

hiiiiiigh dishonors. A vote for me means one-arm driving: one arm on the vheel and the other can go to vaste. A vote for me means plenty of dancing space for every man, child, and Scandinavian in the state of Washington. Too many corns have been hurt on these croooowded dance halls."

Emma's lutefisk speech was persuasive. She said her name was not on the ballot, for some reason, and she did not win the governor's seat. However, "in a couple of places my name was written in anyway."

The candidate. *Emma Repp, pictured in her years as a professional singer. During those years, in the 1930s, she also ran for Washington's governor on the Lutefisk Party ticket.*

Lutefisk
waiting-line
comedian.
Harry Linbeck
(seated) claims
"You gotta
sell the sizzle."

"You gotta BS them all the time," he would say to me in an aside. Then he would turn and boom to the crowd, "Would you people please not eat too much? I haven't eaten yet."

Whenever he used this line, he would draw fire, a bribe offer, or some sort of good-natured shot from the gallery. "You don't care to hit me," he said, smiling. "I've got two canes."

Harry called for applause for a 96-year-old man, declaring that the man's longevity was due, in no small measure, to lutefisk. That got a laugh. Then Harry announced, "You people have not heard this unless you were here last year: The fish is better than ever." He turned to me and said, "You gotta sell the sizzle."

It was time to eat. All I can tell you is I enjoyed another

fine lutefisk meal. Though the meals were starting to run together and I was running out of gas, my appetite for lutefisk never diminished. This worried me. Driving back toward Seattle, I wondered if I would be craving lutefisk tomorrow, and the next day.

However, flying back to Minneapolis the next morning, I realized I had no need to worry. I had been sleepless in Seattle that Sunday evening, and on the plane I wrote in my journal: "Three straight days of lutefisk. Monday after: rumblings in my bowels. A new form of toxic-shock syndrome?"

6

How to Turn Stockfish Into Lutefisk

The daring, do-it-yourself types can do it.

Lutefisk is not easy to love, nor is it easy to make. It may be too much to ask that you do both—love lutefisk and prepare it from stockfish in your own home—but there is nothing wrong with asking, is there?

So, if you try turning stockfish into lutefisk—or even if you try store-bought, ready-to-cook lutefisk—then this chapter will help you avoid the mess ups. You are now going to learn to prepare nothing but firm, flavorful lutefisk.

In the 1930s, '40s, and even the '50s, the art of making lutefisk was not something you learned from a book. Back then, Scandinavian families made lutefisk at home, using recipes passed down but often not written down. Every autumn, families bought stockfish and started soaking it in preparation for a traditional Christmas Eve meal or special event, such as a lutefisk feast for deer-hunting buddies.

With the anticipation of lutefisk came a pleasant tension—one mistake in your soaking process and you ruined the meal. This challenge not only led to an earnest effort, but also to an occasional panicked call to Grandpa and, naturally, a sweeter satisfaction when the fish turned out fine.

Homemade lutefisk.
Mrs. Andrew A. Olson soaks lutefisk at home in St. Paul in
1936. Photo: St. Paul Daily News, *Minnesota Historical Society.*

In the 1950s and '60s, people started to phase out making lutefisk at home. It was a lot of work in a time when
fast foods were starting to infatuate the country. And the
church and the Sons of Norway lodge put on lutefisk din-

ners. There you could see old friends and feel like a part of a community. Attending was almost like voting: You were making a public statement that you valued this tradition and your heritage.

As wonderful as the church and lodge dinners were and are, I maintain that Scandinavians suffered a loss when they stopped making lutefisk at home. The lutefisk-making ritual raised a simple meal to a festive occasion that brought out the best in our families and friends.

I hope we can restore this tradition. I know, this is hardly a universal sentiment. Just the idea of the smell in your house and of taking on more work in a busy holiday season may be overwhelming to you. Fine. However, if you like the nostalgic notion of returning to a ritual that goes back to the roots of your family tree, then read on.

Cod by Odd

When you learn to make lutefisk, you also learn to appreciate fish as a Norwegian or Swede or Finn or Dane does. No matter where you are in Scandinavia, the sea is always nearby—usually a matter of minutes away. The sea influences all of life there—art, literature, economics, politics, and, especially, food.

Odd Unstad of Shoreview, Minn., understands the connection of Scandinavians, fish, and the sea. He was born in 1934 in Smedvik, Norway, and grew up on the Lofoten Islands. As a boy he was always in a boat, fishing. He ate fish six days a week, with meat on Sundays. He came to the United States in 1957.

"Norwegians eat so much fish," says Odd, "and people on the prairie, they are meat people. They don't really know what fish is, although nowadays airlines have made it affordable to get fish in here. But in the old days, what kind of fish did you have up here on the prairie? In the win-

If She Can Do It, You Can Do It

Emma Vatn, 80, has lutefisk twice a week year-round. She makes it herself in her fourth floor condominium in Seattle.

Once a year Emma, a native Norwegian from the Lofoten Islands, picks up 30 pounds of stockfish at the Ballard post office in Seattle. "It comes in a long box, wrapped in brown paper," says her son, Jim Vatn. "The clerk knows us and why we come. 'That smelly fish is out on the loading dock,' he says. They don't bring the box inside."

Emma takes the stockfish home and starts the lutefisk-making process. "She is soaking fish all the time," says Jim. "She has a big tub on her patio."

Whenever family or friends go to Norway, Emma's request is simple: Bring back a box of caustic soda. She uses the soda to make her lye-water soaking solution.

"She doesn't trust the American stuff," says Jim.

Always soaking. *Emma Vatn soaks fish on her fourth-floor condominium patio.*

tertime you didn't have fish. Maybe you ice fished a little bit, but commercially there wasn't much available. So, to the Scandinavians who were brought up by the sea, to have fish here was a glorious occasion."

Nuff said. And now, to the matter at hand—preparing lutefisk. With Odd's guidance, I have broken down the process of soaking, cooking, and serving lutefisk into seven steps.

Seven Steps to Fine Fish

1. Buy the best fish.

Purchase stockfish at least a month before your dinner (stockfish keeps for years in a cool, dry place). Genuine Lofoten cod, says Odd, is best but difficult to find since U.S. lutefisk processors no longer buy it. Odd travels to the Lofotens and brings back cod stockfish.

U.S. lutefisk processors almost always use ling. Ask organizers of a church lutefisk dinner to recommend a processor, or refer to The Lutefisk Dinner Directory for the names, addresses, and telephone numbers of the major lutefisk processors in the United States. In most cases the processor will ship the stockfish to your door.

Your cost is $13 to $17 per pound of ling stockfish (plus shipping), but that figure fluctuates with market changes. Processors wrap the stockfish in plastic and box it for shipping, which takes at least 48 hours. The Day Fish Co. does not ship; you have to go to their retail store in Braham, Minn., which is about 60 miles north of Minneapolis.

New Day Fisheries in Port Townsend, Wash., sells dried, salted cod from Nova Scotia for about $8 per pound (plus shipping).

How much should you order? Olsen Fish Co. president, Bill Andresen, recommends purchasing 2 to 4 pounds of stockfish for a dinner party of 12. The rule of thumb is 1 pound of lutefisk for each dinner guest. Two pounds of stockfish soaks out to about 12 to 14 pounds of lutefisk, but order extra in case some folks come extra hungry.

2. Soak the stockfish in fresh water.

If you can grin and bear the smell, do your soaking in the basement or kitchen. Otherwise, soak the fish in your garage or on the deck or patio.

Fill a large clay crock or galvanized steel wash tub with cold tap water (about 40° F) and submerge the stockfish. You might need to trim the pieces with a carpenter's crosscut saw to make them fit the tub. If so, save the sawdust "to make a wonderful potpourri that will fill your house with the delicious aroma of lutefisk," says Bob Fredell in his booklet, *Lute Koubason's Lutefisk Handbook.*

Do not let the water in your crock or tub freeze. Cover the tub with plywood, which keeps down the smell and keeps out animals and airborne debris.

Odd does something simple to minimize the smell. He soaks his stockfish in a plastic cooler, the kind used on picnics, with the lid closed. This also keeps his Norwegian-English setter, Rex, from the fish. Rex once came bounding down the basement stairs when Odd unwrapped the stockfish. Playfully, Odd leaned a stick of stockfish against a basement pole and made Rex sit. Then he let Rex sniff. "We'll see if he sprinkles on it," Odd said with a wink. "If he does [he did not], we can charge $.50 more per pound."

Let the fish soak in water for five days. Change the water at least every other day. "In the olden days in Norway," says Odd, "they used to put the stockfish in running water, like in the creek. They held the fish in place with a rock."

You can reduce the soaking time by first beating the dry stockfish with a hammer. My feeling is this poor fish has already been through a lot—and the worst is yet to come with the lye bath. Pummeling stockfish strikes me as overkill, and probably does not buy that much time.

One last point about this step: Have faith. After five days of soaking, the stockfish will be a bit bigger, more pliable, and start looking like lutefisk. Imagine, though, the doubt among the first Scandinavians to try this process. Odd says, "We have an old saying in Norway. '*I noden spiste fanden flver*,' which means: 'When the need was greatest, the devil ate flies.'"

Upholding tradition. *Odd Unstad holds up stockfish that he has soaked in water in a plastic cooler.*

Before and after.
Cod stockfish before soaking in water (left) and after.

3. Soak the fish in lye water.

Working with lye scares people—and it should. "This is serious stuff," says Odd. "Lye can be deadly, poisonous, so you have to have respect for it."

I am ultra-cautious with lye. I wear rubber gloves, glasses or safety goggles, a surgical mask or cold weather mask to cover my mouth and nose—whatever it takes to protect my skin, eyes, nose, and mouth. If lye splashes on me, I wash it off immediately with water. I have eyewash ready, and I would not hesitate to call 911.

I can buy a 12-ounce plastic tub of Lewis Red Devil Lye crystals for about $2 at a building supply or hardware store. Lye is also called caustic soda, which is sodium hydroxide (NaOH). *Make sure you buy lye that is suitable for use with food.* (See "Warnings About Lye" on page 107.)

When learning about lye soaking, consult with someone who is experienced in processing lutefisk from stockfish (see "Lutefisk Processors" on page 174). If you have *any* doubts, stop and simply buy lutefisk at grocery stores.

There are many formulas for making lye solutions. I rely on Odd's: Mix 0.6 ounces of lye for each gallon of water.

"This is science now," Odd says, using a calculator to determine that 7.5 gallons of water (amount he will add to his soaking cooler) requires 4.5 ounces of lye crystals, which he weighs on a small food scale. Odd uses a stick to stir the crystals into a quart-size plastic pail of water. The lye fizzes and the pail feels warm from the chemical reaction.

Now you can run cold water into the soaking tub or cooler, add the lye solution, and submerge the stockfish.

Soak the fish in the lye solution for about five days, stirring daily.

"To make lutefisk is an art," Odd says. That's another way of saying you must keep an eye on the lutefisk because the lye-soaking process time varies by a day more or less, depending on how quickly the lye breaks down protein into amino acids. The thumb test tells you when the fish is ready: The filet has a squishy, gel-like consistency you can penetrate with your thumb.

One more note about this step: Odd does not skin his Lofoten cod. Soaking skinless stockfish speeds the process, so, again, check the fish daily using the thumb test.

4. Soak fish in fresh water
for 10 to 14 days, until firm.

Now that you have gone to all this work of putting lye into the fish, you must take it back out. Remove the fish and

Boy Falls Into Lye

No lie. James R. Hawkinson once took a quick lye bath.

Hawkinson has blocked many of the details, but he believes this trauma occurred in Chicago in the 1930s when he was 7 or 8 years old. He recalls leaving the kitchen to go outside to play. Between the kitchen and porch was a hallway, where Hawkinson's mother had placed a galvanized-steel wash tub full of lye water. She was soaking stockfish for the Christmas meal of lutfisk (Swedes use this spelling), brown beans, Swedish meatballs, and ham.

He backed into the kitchen door to open it, then continued to back down the hall. He tripped on the tub and fell into lye water, about a foot deep.

"I don't think I was in it very long," recalls Hawkinson, who now lives in White Bear Lake, Minn. He yelled, and his mother immediately stripped his clothes and washed him thoroughly. The fish was slimy—he does remember that.

Though he says he suffered no after-effects, he adds, "You never know, it may have been the shot that protected me from a lot of things."

The dip did not affect his affection for lutfisk: "I was never terribly fond of it. I could not tell if it was going down or coming up when I ate it."

Warnings About Lye

Here is good advice about working with lye, from Putting Food By *by Ruth Hertzberg, Beatrice Vaughan, and Janet Greene.*

Lye can become activated in the presence of only the moisture in the air on a muggy day. It is highly caustic. The antidote for searing contact is to slosh immediately with cold water and follow with a boric-acid solution (eyes) or vinegar.

If you buy household lye/caustic soda, make sure it is suitable for use with food. It should be designated as "lye" or "lycons" on the container and contain no aluminum, nitrates, or stabilizers. Do not use commercial drain openers, either crystalline or liquid.

Use only enamel- or granite-ware pots or kettles. Never use utensils of aluminum; aluminum reacts violently with lye in water.

Ready to cook. *After soaking in water to remove most of the lye, this filet is ready for cooking. "Each filet feeds four Americans —or one Norwegian," says Odd.*

dispose of the lye water. Odd simply flushes it down the toilet—the lye water, not the fish.

Rinse the tub or cooler and fill it with fresh water. Soak the fish for 10 to 14 days. Change water daily for the first five days, then every other day. You can also put the fish in a basin beneath slowly running water for part of the time. The fish loses most of the lye—and, mercifully, the smell— in this soaking, and it gains more size. Odd says soaking longer than two weeks causes the filets to become too firm.

The Ethnic Defense

New Day Fisheries, a lutefisk processor in Port Townsend, Wash., uses hydrochloric acid to neutralize lye water before discharging it. That's the word from Bob Miller, New Day's quality control manager.

"The wastewater treatment plant will call you on it," he says. "If your discharge is too high in base because of the lye, it corrodes the pipes. If it is too high in acid [from too much hydrochloric acid], it is hard on the microorganisms in the treatment plant."

Miller said health inspectors occasionally will pop in and look at the foamy vats of fish in lye water. "They'll say, 'What the hell is that?' I tell them it's an ethnic thing, leave it alone. People don't die from it.' They never get back to me."

5. Soak it in salt water for a day or two.

This is not a necessary step, but this salt soaking may help firm up the fish just the way you like it.

If your dinner is four or more days away, cut the filets into meal-size chunks and put them into plastic bags for freezing. Odd does not like to freeze the fish, but sometimes he has to. "In Norway, we used to store the fish in holes dug near the bottom of a 4-foot snowdrift," he says.

If dinner is a day or two away, let the filets soak in water that is lightly salted. A little salt adds flavor, draws out more lye, and keeps the fish firm but not too firm.

Your finished, soaked-out product should have swelled up to six to eight times the size of the original filet. "Each filet feeds four Americans—or one Norwegian," says Odd.

6. Boil, bake, or microwave
lutefisk until flaky.

If you like extra-firm fish, put the chunks in salted water for two hours before cooking. Remember to rinse in cold water and let the fish soak in fresh water for about 10 minutes.

Remove the filets from the water. If you are using cod, pull or cut out the backbone and cut the filets into 4- to 6-inch square chunks. With ling, just cut the filets. Trim off fins, tail, unsightly spots, and the area around the gills, but do not remove the skin. Skin holds the fish together during cooking and, therefore, helps prevent the meat from turning quickly to mush (and your name to mud). Observe the color of the fish. It should be white with a hint of blue-green. The brown or darker spots, says Odd, means the lye did not affect that area much. The area is usually small, so cut it out.

Here are several methods for cooking lutefisk. Whatever way you use, do not overcook. Always check lutefisk before the cooking time is up. The fish is done when the meat segments start to separate. The pros describe done lutefisk as when the meat starts to "flake easily." When the fish is done, drain the broth and serve.

Microwaving

Place lutefisk skin-side down on microwaveable pan. Cover and cook on high for about 12 minutes, turning the pan a half turn after 8 minutes.

Baking

Preheat oven to 350 degrees. Place lutefisk, skin down, in large glass baking dish. Bake 30 minutes.

Or preheat oven to 375 degrees. Salt fish with 1 to 2 teaspoons per pound. Place skin-side down on aluminum foil, fold foil over fish, crimp edges together, and with a fork poke holes in the bottom of the foil to let broth flow out. Put wrapped fish in an ovenproof glass dish and bake 30 to 40 minutes. Again, check before the time is up. Some cooks say the foil prevents the fish from becoming too dry.

Boiling—the old fashioned way

To a large stainless-steel kettle, add enough water to boil all the lutefisk you have prepared. Add ¼ cup of salt per quart of water.

Some people put the fish in the salt water and cook until the brine just starts to boil, usually 10 to 20 minutes (more fish means longer boiling time). Remove the kettle from the burner and skim off any foam on the surface of the salt water. Let the fish stand uncovered for 5 to 10 minutes, until flaky, and serve at once.

I prefer Odd's way of cooking lutefisk: Bring brine to rolling boil, then add lutefisk chunks. This causes the boiling to stop temporarily. Bring the brine back to a boil and remove the kettle from the heat. The fish should be starting to flake. Let lutefisk stand in brine until serving. Odd says you can let the fish stand for 30 minutes, but he usually serves within 10 to 15 minutes after removing it from the heat. He pulls the fish from the brine, and serves it on a tray.

Many cooks at church dinners like to skin the filets before boiling. Skinless fish falls apart easily, so these cooks boil their lutefisk in cheesecloth bags. Some people say cheesecloth makes it hard to see if the fish is done. But Gus Bjorlee swears by cheesecloth bags. He has used them since 1976, when he started cooking lutefisk for the Sons of Norway dinner in Bremerton, Wash. "You can tell the fish is done by just lifting up the bag and hitting it," he says. "You don't want it to where it feels soft. That's not good."

To see if the fish is done, you can also poke through the cheesecloth with a fork. "The fish is done when the fork doesn't stick," says Dick Lone, a cook for the Norse Glee Club lutefisk dinner in Sioux Falls, S.D. "It will turn to wallpaper paste if you wait too long."

All cooks tell you that boiling gets the fish close to done, but letting the fish stand finishes the job. "Here's a little secret" if you use cheesecloth, says Gus: "Take the fish out before it's done. Put it in the steamer [a covered pot], where it drains and the meat separates and falls away so nicely."

Terry Schlosser, a cook at the Lions Club lutefisk dinner in Stanwood, Wash., uses a unique homemade steamer. After boiling the fish, he lifts the bags into a big baker's mixing bowl, which sits atop a garbage can. Broth drains from the bags through holes drilled in the bottom of the mixing bowl. All the while the steam continues to cook the fish. When the fish is done, he drains the water using a specially installed spigot at the bottom of the garbage can.

The important point with cooking lutefisk is to be vigilant. Whatever method you use, pay attention to the fish. When it starts to flake, turn off the heat and let it stand. Jon Gullixson, a cook for the Idun Lodge 5–074 lutefisk dinner put on by the Dane County Grieg Male Chorus in Madison, Wis., puts it this way: "When it gets to that point of flaking out, don't play another hand of seven-card stud. Get to the stove and don't leave. If the phone rings, let it ring, because the lutefisk is ready."

7. Serve it hot with potatoes and other plain, good foods.

At long last your lutefisk is ready. Remove the skin right before serving if you like. Cod skin peels off easily; ling not so easily. Garnish with parsley and lemon slices, then serve with boiled potatoes.

Patent pending?
Terry Schlosser, in Stanwood, Wash., shows how he uses his steamer, made from a garbage can, to finish cooking the lutefisk.

"Use Idaho potatoes, which are the mealy type," says Odd. "Potatoes are almost as important as the lutefisk. If you don't have good potatoes, you'll ruin the lutefisk."

Also serve flatbread and rutabagas (or carrots, peas, or corn). Odd mashes his boiled rutabagas and mixes in salt, pepper, brown sugar, and pieces of cooked carrots. Ummm.

Serve any or all of the following: lefse, lingonberries, cranberries, *rømmegrøt,* cake, ice cream, *krumkake,* rosettes, *sandbakkels, aquavit,* beer, wine, milk, and coffee.

Melted butter is a must if you are Norwegian; cream sauce, if you are Swedish. Or try a tasty mustard sauce. Odd makes a knock-out sauce of chopped, sautéed onions mixed with bacon fat and crumbled bacon.

Though meatballs are not a must, they are often served to those who tense up when given lutefisk. "Meatballs soften the blow," says Odd. When my wife, Jane, and I went to Odd's lutefisk dinner for the first time, he asked me about Jane's position on lutefisk. I said she stood firmly

Lifelong lutefisk epicure. Odd dons a lutefisk chef's hat, made by friends.

against it. He understood. He has heard this before from other heathens, and therefore, he would serve meatballs. However, he had this message for Jane: "You tell her that this will be her conversion night!" As it turned out, it was — sort of. She loved Odd's cod lutefisk. She is still working on the ling lutefisk served by the churches and lodges.

Finishing Touches

Odd's lutefisk dinners are good examples of how to do it right. Here are a few hosting tidbits I garnered as a guest at his festive affairs.

1. Bring out your best china, silverware, and crystal. Iron your finest tablecloth. Light the candles. This is a big deal here.

2. Invite only the converted, or at least folks for whom there is hope that they will see the light about lutefisk. You do not want to go through weeks of preparation only to have some stick-in-the-mud stick his or her nose up at your fare. Odd's guests are usually from a group of 40 Norwegian-born friends, whom he has been honoring with this meal since 1982.

3. Have a story to tell. Baard Thue, one of Odd's dinner guests, told how his grandmother in Norway stored birch ashes near the hearth and used these ashes for making lye to make lutefisk. At another dinner Tove Corbett talked about living in Oslo, Norway, during World War II when food was sometimes scarce. "But lutefisk was sent from relatives outside of Oslo," she recalled. "It had to be cured and cooked, and it seemed fresh. We ate so much of it, though, that I got sick of it and did not eat it for years. Then in the last 15 years or so, it became a big deal to eat lutefisk again."

4. Have a joke to tell. If it's a little raunchy, that's okay —

Candlelight and good friends—a must at lutefisk dinners.
Ingrid Slettemoen and Bjarne Mathisen
are regular guests at Odd's dinner table.

if you tell it with style and dignity. No one can tell a joke
like Odd and his Norwegian friends. They clang their gob-
lets (often in need of a refill), stand up, and turn a two-
minute joke into a 12-minute saga. The punch line is
simply an epilogue because there are so many laughs along
the way. An expression here, an editorial diversion there,
and exchanges with listeners who cannot contain their
brilliance—these all bring on chuckles.

At one dinner Patrick Corbett told this Ole and Lena
joke: Ole is noticing that Lena has put on weight, maybe
from eating too much lutefisk. One day Ole is crabby and
tells Lena that her back side is getting as broad as a Weber
kettle grill. Lena lets it pass—for now. Come Saturday
night, Ole is in an amorous mood and suggests to Lena
that they go to the bedroom to make beautiful music together. Lena, she thinks about this, then says with a smile,

"Why Ole, you don't think I would heat up my big grill for one little weenie, do you?"

5. End the dinner with a toast. It should be heartfelt and eloquent, and a lutefisk dinner is not limited to one toast. These Norwegians enjoy a soliloquy. Mark Antony and William Jennings Bryan had nothing on them.

In truth, the toasts are moving testimonies to long friendships. Odd then brings the wonderful meal to a close with a response that is true to his Scandinavian ways: "In Norway, they have an expression: 'Taste and well-being can never be discussed.'"

7

Lutefisk Humor

Where there's a smell, there's a laugh.

Many lutefisk lovers would have me end right here. Don't bother getting into all that lutefisk humor, which, they say, stretches the bounds of humor's definition. Humor is something that makes you laugh, but some of these lutefisk jokes make you cry with disgust.

For example, there's the one that says cod has not always been eaten in the form of lutefisk. Centuries ago, Scandinavians tried to *smoke* fish but were not successful.

They could not figure out which *end to light. . . .* This bit of humor is from *The Lutefisk Handbook: A Humorous Look at the World's Most Misunderstood Fish,* by David Jones and Norman Hildrum.

The laugh-no-more-at-lutefisk lobbyists claim that humor needs to have an element of reality to it. Writer E. B. White said, "Humor plays close to the big hot fire that is truth." The "joke" above is, therefore, not humor because everyone understands a true Scandinavian knows which end of a cod to light. (Now *that's* a joke!)

Many Scandinavians appeal for balance with lutefisk. Okay, have a laugh or two at lutefisk's expense, but then give it a rest. Why keep beating a dead fish? These people treasure their fish and want to hose down lutefisk jokesters when they start getting too lathered up.

For example, in Seattle, I picked up the Oct. 27, 1995, copy of the *Western Viking* newspaper. A letter to the editor from an Alaskan writer tries to get cute by making leftover lutefisk a hazardous-waste issue. The letter is signed "Lee F. Olson, President-for-life, NAAOJ (National Association for the Alimination of Oley Jokes)."

The editor, Alf Lunder Knudsen, Ph.D., responds: "It is the time of year for lutefisk jokes, unfortunately. Most of them are poor—or is it simply, in poor taste? In the meantime, some of us enjoy our lutefisk and are happy that there still are people seeking employment/enjoyment cooking up bad tasting lutefisk jokes."

Right on, Alf!

And then there is Bill Andresen, president of Olsen Fish Co. in Minneapolis, the largest lutefisk processor in the world. When the *Today* show came to Minneapolis for a few shows, Andresen arranged to have Jane Pauley served lutefisk on the air. "She wouldn't touch the stuff," says Andresen with a smile. "The woman has no taste."

Not so amused. *Alf Lunder Knudsen, editor of a Norwegian-American newspaper, says the lutefisk "humor comes up short, usually."*

People who overdo it on lutefisk humor also have no taste, says Andresen. "I can remember growing up with that kind of humor," he says. "There are the jokes about putting stockfish outside the store and the dogs would come along and leave their mark on the fish. And how it's indestructible. Well, bull! It's like any other kind of food; you got to treat it right. Just keep the humor out of it.

"You laugh along, and it becomes a part of selling your product. But I've thought, gee whiz, I'm going to get on a competing radio station three months out of the year and tell bad stories about Boone and Erickson [announcers on WCCO radio in Minneapolis], who have made a living knocking lutefisk. That's no lie.

"I don't like the humor because it is always derogatory. It does nothing for us. I tell you, last fall I called my lawyer. I'm coming back from a wedding one night down near the airport, and here's a big billboard showing a fifth of whiskey. The caption says 'Lutefisk Helper.' What an insult

A movement is afoot to enact the so-called "dumb jokes" law in states where people commonly eat lutefisk. Generally speaking, the law would require people to balance each bad comment about lutefisk with a good one, in the interest of equal time.

The state where passage of this law is most likely is Wisconsin. After all, in 1995 Rep. Scott Jensen worked heroically to repeal what he called "dumb laws" still buried in the statutes. According to an Associated Press report, one dumb law specifically exempted lutefisk from the definition of "toxic substance" under the state's toxic substances right-to-know laws.

Perhaps Rep. Jensen might work with equal zeal on a "dumb jokes" law. Specifically, the law would limit the number of lutefisk cracks to, say, six per person per lutefisk dinner season (October through March). After bagging your six, you must praise lutefisk each time you slam it. Failure to comply leads to a penalty of eating 1 pound of lutefisk per joke that is not coupled with a compliment.

Wait! Stop the presses! I have just opened my mail and now have serious doubts that Wisconsin will ever have a "dumb jokes" law. It appears I have sadly mis-

Your Fish Today?

judged my neighbors to the east. I have heard rumors—and this letter confirms it—that when lutefisk is "in the water," Wisconsin bad-humor sharks start circling. The letter is from Pastor Jerry A. Olson, from Christ Lutheran Church in DeForest, Wis. He encloses copies of two newspaper stories he "provoked to feed the lutefisk frenzy," he writes. The stationary bears this letterhead: "Proud to Live in America, a Norwegian Colony Since 1004 A.D."

The articles, which promote the church's annual lute-fisk dinner in November, explain how the church had built a lutefisk "blind" for catching the wily lutefisk running in the Yahara River. One of the stories, this one in the DeForest Times-Tribune, *shows photos of two men in a duck blind—wearing blindfolds, presumably to protect their identity because they could not possibly see to catch fish. Another photo shows three men demonstrating a new, church-endorsed, twin-pronged lutefisk rod, designed to speed up catching the 3,000 pounds of lutefisk needed for the church dinner.*

It is clear these good folks can't help themselves. A "dumb jokes" law pertaining to lutefisk will never fly in Wisconsin.

to all the Lutheran congregations we sell to every year. Stuff like that just drives me nuts."

To show he has a sense of humor about lutefisk humor, Andresen pulls out a yellowed copy of *The Wall Street Journal,* dated Dec. 14, 1982. He points to a front-page story titled, "Some People Hold Lutefisk in Esteem; Others Hold Noses." The article gives his product a fair shake, describing lutefisk and what it means to Scandinavians. It throws in a few predictable digs, quoting folks who gag on this "Norwegian Jell-O." But the story said Julia Child gave lutefisk her blessing, as long as it had a sauce. One Norwegian immigrant was quoted as saying, "There is nothing as good as lutefisk or as bad as lutefisk. If it's made wrong, it becomes like jelly, like man-of-war out of the ocean, soft and ishy. If it's made right, it's more firm."

The Lutefisk Stamp

Some are born to lutefisk, some achieve lutefisk, and some—like Les Kouba—have lutefisk thrust upon them.

Kouba, a Minneapolis wildlife artist, was minding his own business one December morning in 1993, when he got stuck making a lutefisk stamp.

"The day was typical for Minnesota, cold and clear as a bell," recalls Kouba. He turned on WCCO radio while doing some paperwork. Announcers Charlie Boone and Roger Erickson were clowning around about how someone should make a Lutefisk Unlimited stamp, kinda like a Ducks Unlimited stamp. Kouba remembers them saying "in their typical fun-loving way, 'We're going to get our friend Les Kouba to design a lutefisk stamp.' I did a double-take. Hell, I didn't know a thing about lutefisk."

Pretty soon Kouba's phone started to ring: "They asked, 'When can I get one of those lutefisk stamps, Les?' I must have received about 1,000 calls over the next few weeks." He told them the work was in progress and that he would get back to them.

The only progress Kouba had made that morning was deciding to seize the day and make a lutefisk stamp. He painted the stamp, and then he and a friend, Bob Fredell, produced the Lute Koubason's Lutefisk Handbook. *The booklet sells for $3.50, the stamp for $5, and a 16" x 16" framed print and stamp for $110. For more information write Lutefisk Unlimited, 926 Plymouth Building, Minneapolis, MN 55402. Or call 612-338-7247.*

Proceed With Caution

With respect to lutefisk loyalists who ask that we limit ourselves when lambasting lutefisk, I proceed with some lutefisk jokes.

Please keep in mind that almost by definition, lutefisk jokes—but *not* lutefisk itself—are bad. However, speaking for myself anyway, there are times when bad is good, especially with humor. That is, something odd or a bit twisted in my makeup likes these lutefisk jokes.

And so, I have gleaned the following jokes from here and there, and present you with the best of the bad. Read at your own risk.

From Red Stangland's *Norwegian Home Companion:* "Our dog got hold of some lutefisk the other day. He spent the next four days licking himself, trying to get rid of the taste." ... "Lena says that Ole's favorite sandwich is a BLT. Baloney, lutefisk, and torsk." ... "The Norwegian asked the Dane if he ever ate lutefisk. The Dane said no, he hadn't, but he thought he stepped in some one time." ... "What are the usual door prizes at a Norwegian wedding? Second prize, a night with the bride. First prize, 50 pounds of lutefisk."

From *The Best of Queen Lena* by Charlene Power: "Lena was sick, so Ole took her to the doctor, who prescribed a trip to the beach for some ocean air. Instead, Ole, who was very thrifty, stayed at home and fanned her with a lutefisk."

And these from the aforementioned *The Lutefisk Handbook* by Jones and Hildrum: "The good news is lutefisk makes you stronger. The bad news? Smell isn't everything." ... A quote from Richard Nixon: "Don't ask me to make lutefisk. I am not a cook."

And finally these two from *101 More Things to Do With Lutefisk* by Ed Fischer: "Weird fact: A Scandinavian tribe in northern Norway once used lutefisk for money. They were the most frugal people ever known to man."..."Sven Torgleson of Ollie, Minn., says that when his son acts up at a lutefisk meal, he's sent to his room *with* supper."

So, there you have it. I must say that I suffered so much exposure to these bad jokes that I have made up two of my own to include in this chapter. Stuff like this: "Italians use dried stockfish to make delicious dishes. What did the Italian, in Minnesota on business, say when he stopped by a lutefisk processing plant and saw lutefisk soaking in a tub? 'THAT'S A LYE!'" And this one: "How are Mae West and lutefisk alike: When they're good, they're very, very good. But when they're bad, they get mushy."

Enough. Looking back on this section with objectivity, it appears my efforts to "raise the bar," to improve the quality of lutefisk jokes, have failed. On to poetry.

The Poetry of Lutefisk

Lutefisk, without a doubt, has moved people. (Yeah, to fresh air. Sorry.) In my research I have found that lutefisk has moved people to such passion that they scribble down verse on the backs of lefse rounds at lutefisk dinners. If indeed "poetry is trouble dunked in tears," as Gwyn Thomas wrote, then lutefisk poetry is trouble dunked in lye.

Love That Lutefisk

They salt and air-dry cod fish
Till it's like a two-by-four
Then they soak the fish in lye a week,
Then rinse, and soak some more.

The smell of soaking lutefisk,
As it wafts across the fjord
Can ruin TV reception and
Pop knotholes from a board.

But Norsemen love their lutefisk;
And they can hardly wait,
To take it from the lye barrel
And put it on their plate.

In truth it takes a true Norseman,
To eat a cod so soaked;
For lesser men have held their nose
And eaten it, and croaked.
—from Leftover Lutefisk *by Art Lee*
originally appeared in the Iola *(Wis.)* Herald

O Lutefisk

(May be sung to "O Tannenbaum")
O Lutefisk ... O Lutefisk ... how fragrant your aroma
O Lutefisk ... O Lutefisk ... You put me in a coma.
You smell so strong ... you look like glue
You taste yust like an overshoe
But lutefisk ... come Saturday
I tink I'll eat you anyvay.

O Lutefisk ... O Lutefisk ... I put you by the door vay
I vanted you to ripen up ... yust like dey do in Norvay
A dog came by and sprinkled you ...
I hit him vid an army shoe
O Lutefisk ... now I suppose
I'll eat you as I hold my nose.

O Lutefisk ... O Lutefisk ... how vell I do remember
On Christmas Eve how we'd receive ...
Our big treat of December
It vasn't turkey or fried ham ...
It vasn't even pickled spam
My mudder knew dere vas no risk ...
In serving buttered lutefisk.

O Lutefisk ... O Lutefisk ... now everyone discovers
Dat Lutefisk and lefse makes ...
Norvegians better lovers
Now all da vorld can have a ball ...
you're better dan dat Yeritol
O Lutefisk ... vid brennevin [Norwegian brandy]
You make me feel like Errol Flynn.
  —*by Red Stangland*

Doug Setterberg and Stan Borenson sang a lutefisk song, "I Want To Go Where The Wild Goose Goes," on their album *Cold, Cold Heart (and other 'TORCH' songs)*. This duo recorded "Just a Little Lefse Will Go a Long Way," which I mentioned in *The Last Word on Lefse*. So it is only fitting that they make an appearance in this book, with a sampling of the lyrics to the chorus and one verse.

(Chorus)
I vant to go where the lutefisk go,
So I yump in a boat and I row and I row
Herrings, sardines, and mackerel, too,
They don't taste good like a lutefisk dooooooooooo.

(First verse)
Last night I heard a lutefisk burp
Svimming around in the bay like a yerk.
I tried to sleep but I couldn't do that
So I'm gonna eat fish til I'm good and fat.

Lutefisk Lament (selected stanzas)

From out in the kitchen an odor came stealing
That fairly set my senses to reeling
The smell of Lutefisk creeped down the hall
And wilted a plant, in a pot, on the wall
The others reacted as though they were smitten
While the aroma laid low my small helpless kitten
Uncle Oscar and Lars said "Oh, that smell yummy"
And Kermit's eye glittered while he patted his tummy
The scent skipped off the ceiling and bounced off the door
And the bird in the Cuckoo Clock fell on the floor. …

Then came to my plate and to my fevered brain
There seemed enough Lutefisk to derail a train
It looked like a mountain of congealing glue
Oddly transparent, yet discolored in hue
With butter and cream sauce I tried to conceal it

I salted and peppered, but the smell would reveal it
I drummed up my courage, I tried to be bold
Mama reminds me to eat before it gets cold
I decided to face it, "Uff da," I sighed
"Uff da, indeed," my stomach replied.

Then I summoned that resolve for which our breed
   is known
My hand took the fork as with a mind of its own
And with reckless abandon that Lutefisk I ate
Within 20 seconds I'd cleaned up my plate
Uncle Kermit flashed me an ear-to-ear grin
As butter and cream sauce dripped from his chin
Then, to my great shock, he whispered in my ear
"I'm sure glad this is over for another year."

It was then that I learned a great and wonderful truth
That Swedes and Norwegians from old men to youth
Must each pay their dues to have the great joy
Of being known as a good Scandahoovian boy
And so to you all, as you face the great test
Happy Christmas to you, and to you all my best.
   — by Don Freeburg

Da Blue-Eyed Lutefisk by Arthur C. Stavig is a poem I pondered. In the end I decided it was too sad to include in this inspiring collection. It's about a guy who bought a fish for making lutefisk. The fish had blue eyes and looked like his Uncle Knute. He couldn't cut up the fish—"Ay couldn't stan' tew see him cook/Ven dose eyes vas vatching me!"—so he gave away the fish, and he and the wife ate sardines for Christmas. An important work, to be sure, bringing balance and a mournful reality to what critics say is the normally la-la world of lutefisk.

   The following poem I picked up at a lutefisk dinner put

on by the Norwegian Glee Club of Minneapolis. That night, the club did not sing this to the tune of "Mickey Mouse," but you can.

Lutefisk March

What's the best food you can eat?
And good for you and me?
Kills the germs and makes you look
Better for your age.

If you think you've had it bad,
this fisk has had it worse.
Died and dried and soaked in lye
To make your buttons burst!

Lutefisk, Lutefisk
Forever let us hold our Lefse high!
Come al-long and sing a song and join the fam-i-ly!
L-U-T, L-U-T, E-F-I-S-K!
— *by Robert G. (Sven) Olson*

Finally, I too have been moved by lutefisk to write verse, and I humbly offer these three poems, all inspired by the smell of lutefisk.

If It Wasn't for the Smell

If it wasn't for the smell
Would we come together quite as well?
If we couldn't wince at that fragrance
That puts some people in a trance
And makes some others want to dance
Would lutefisk dinners ever gel?

Oh, yes, I know that odor
Makes some people want to motor.
But you are zealous 'bout this fish
Deep down, you won't say that it's ish
Your nose says "No," your heart says "Go"
So tell the gang, "Move over!"

Loyal

We come for the lutefisk, leave with the smell
One is more loyal, which one, can you tell?
The fare that is there and gone in a bite
Or the smell that stays with you all through the night
And the days and the weeks and months and the years
A true friend that ignores your disdain and your fears,
Amused by your digs, so patient and true
'Til you sit with that past that is certainly you.

The Yell of Lutefisk

Our senses yearn to tell
And such it is with smell.
With lutefisk
Sometimes the smell
Does more for us
Than tell—it yells!

The yell, for some, can mean "Steer clear!"
For others, it is but a cheer:
"We're here! Let's eat!
All's well!
All's well!"
Thank lutefisk and our sense of yell.

Lutefisk Bumper Stickers

Bumper stickers are often bold, sometimes bilious, and sometimes just plain bonkers. They allow you to say things that come from your gut—and sometimes from your head—without any back talk. Bumper stickers are hit-and-run, and they often have a "take-that" tone to them. About the nicest one I saw was in the parking lot of Mount Olivet Lutheran Church in Minneapolis during the church's December lutefisk dinner: GRACE HAPPENS. Even this bumper sticker is a positive response to the more popular but less positive sticker: SPIT HAPPENS (typo intended).

Give lutefisk bumper stickers their due, however: They do not stoop to sass and brass. They are upbeat, friendly, respectful—like these I found in The Lutefisk Handbook:

> *HONK! IF YOU LOVE LUTEFISK*
>
> *CAUTION! THIS VEHICLE BRAKES*
> *FOR LUTEFISK SUPPERS*
>
> *LUTEFISK LOVERS DO IT WITH MELTED BUTTER*

To this list I add my own lutefisk bumper stickers:

> *LUTEFISK—ANOTHER WHITE LYE!*
>
> *LUTEFISK—ONCE PAST MY NOSE,*
> *FOREVER CURLS MY TOES*
>
> *LUTEFISK—SEE WHAT HAPPENS*
> *WHEN YOU LYE TO COD?*
>
> *BE BRAVE—EAT LUTEFISK*
>
> *LUTEFISK—NONE BUT THE BRAVE*
> *DESERVES THE FARE*

LUTEFISK—TO EAT IS HUMAN, TO DIGEST IS DIVINE

*LUTEFISK CHURCH DINNERS—WALK BY FAITH,
NOT BY SMELL*

*HOPE FOR GOOD LUTEFISK
BUT PREPARE FOR THE WORST*

*NATURE, TIME, AND LUTEFISK
ARE THE THREE GREAT PHYSICIANS*

*LAZARUS LOVED LUTEFISK—
BOTH CAME BACK FROM THE DEAD*

*SHAKESPEARE ON LUTEFISK: SOMETHING IS
ROTTEN IN THE STATE OF DENMARK*

LUTEFISK—MY ZEAL HATH CONSUMED ME

MELVILLE'S LUTEFISK MASTERPIECE—MOBY ICK

*THE MORE I SEE LUTEFISK,
THE MORE I LIKE SPINACH*

KISSING DOESN'T LAST, LUTEFISK DOES

LYE DETECTOR—SOMEONE WHO SMELLS LUTEFISK

LUTEFISK—JUST DO IT

FLATTERY AND LUTEFISK—OK IF YOU DON'T INHALE

*IF I HAD LIFE TO LIVE AGAIN,
I'D EAT LUTEFISK SOONER*

THE MAN WHO MARRIES FOR LUTEFISK EARNS IT

*LUTEFISK DOES NOT BUILD CHARACTER—
IT REVEALS IT*

*LUTEFISK—FOR A DESPERATE DISEASE,
A DESPERATE CURE*

LUTEFISK—FOLLOW YOUR BLISS . . . AND YOUR NOSE

KNOWLEDGE COMES BUT LUTEFISK LINGERS

The Columnists

Every holiday season, the merry air around lutefisk hits the papers. In cities and towns where Scandinavians live, newspapers regularly announce upcoming church lutefisk suppers and run features that chronicle the preparations. Columnists here and there will look to lutefisk to rescue them during the holidays, to pull them and their readers from the usual news of trouble in the world toward something bright and festive. So they write about lutefisk.

Clearly, they have fun with their lutefisk pieces. Take Bill Wundram, of the *Quad-City Times* in Davenport, Iowa, for example. I received four of his columns from my mom, Darlene Schumacher, who lived in Bettendorf, Iowa, with my stepfather, Hank Schumacher. In his travels Wundram had wandered into a lutefisk dinner at the First Lutheran Church in Blooming Prairie, Minn. He wrote it up in a cheerful column, and to his surprise, received many responses during the next couple months.

Readers' tales of lutefisk became fodder for three more of Wundram's columns. He wrote of Kent Olson from Davenport, who told about how people honk at his Iowa "LUTEFSK" personalized license plates (Iowa only allowed seven letters). Gene Gibbons of Rock Island, Ill., remembered lutefisk and his days as a school principal: "One of my assistant principals, a Swede, would on occasion invite me to share a lutefisk lunch with him. The lutefisk smelled so foul that we had to eat it on the 50-yard line, in the middle of the football field. Any closer to the school and they would have to dismiss classes." Rune Oberg of Moline, Ill., told Wundram: "My mom used to fix it. She'd go out in the woods and bring back a nice, sticky slab of pine. It had to be plenty sticky, with the sap oozing out. Mom'd put the lutefisk on the slab of wood and bake it for 20 minutes. Then, we'd throw out the lutefisk and eat the slab of wood."

Another columnist who talks lutefisk is George Hesselberg of the *Wisconsin State Journal* in Madison. When it comes to slamming lutefisk, he does so playfully and with restraint, perhaps because he is sensitive to receiving hate mail. In response to one of his harsher lutefisk columns, Hesselberg once received a letter that began with the salutation "Dear Satan." At the end of another lutefisk column he applauds his own restraint, asking the readers if they noticed he had "not said what the stuff looks like when it is ready to be eaten? (This is a morning newspaper. People are eating breakfast while reading this.)"

He continues, "Notice how I have not told my favorite (true) story about dried fish, the story about the tons of dried fish shipped from Norway" to a country that "did not realize it was fish until after it rained. The dried fish had been used for roof shingles.

"No, you won't hear any badmouthing of lutefisk from this corner.

"If there is one thing lutefisk does for you, it teaches you restraint."

This is the same column, by the way, that led with this joke. "In Viking times, you knew you were going to have a bad day if you woke up in your little village and smelled lutefisk, because it meant the Viking ships were only about 10 miles away."

The teller of the joke was none other than our friend and president of Olsen Fish Co., Bill Andresen. See, Bill does have a sense of humor about lutefisk.

Over the years, Jim Klobuchar of the *Star Tribune* in Minneapolis has written innumerable good lines about lutefisk. In applauding the Norwegians for staging a beautiful 1994 Winter Olympics, Klobuchar said that Minnesota Norwegians can proudly "come out of the closet." He qualified this by adding "that Minnesota Norwegians have not exactly gone underground. As long as it is legal to eat torsk and lutefisk in Minnesota without insurance coverage, Norwegians will be visible."

Lucille Johnson of Edina, Minn., sent me a Klobuchar column about one Everett Larson, who was preparing to fly from sunny Florida to Minnesota solely for a lutefisk dinner. "We have testimony from this man's friends and relatives to the effect that Everett Larson is in full command of his brain cells. He did not lose an election or quarrel with his wife. He is not having trouble with his lower tubes, which most rational people consider the only acceptable reason for eating lutefisk. …

"Where I was born on the Iron Range of northern Minnesota, lutefisk is practically unknown except for an occasional use as a remedy for communicable disease. It is a two-way attack on my nostrils and stomach. I still need a doctor's permission to eat in dining rooms where lutefisk is served."

In another column Klobuchar said he had gotten wind of someone trying to host a Lutefisk Bowl between the two worst teams in college football. Support was needed from the heavy hitters in the Twin Cities, many of them Scandinavians, Klobuchar said. "The historic suspicions between Norwegians and Swedes are broad and well-deserved. There is only one subject on which the most fanatical of the Norwegians and Swedes agree, and that is the ambrosial qualities of lutefisk."

Could a Lutefisk Bowl really fly? Klobuchar asks. He answers: "It could. I'm convinced of it and scared … [because of] the clout of the lutefisk underground.

"Listen. Some of the biggest persuaders in town eat lutefisk, most of them on the sly. You've got the top shelf in banking, stock brokering, and real estate, people who could make the Lutefisk Bowl happen. ... The truth is that these shakers often go to little out-of-the-way gatherings to eat their lutefisk, where they cannot be identified. Hundreds of them do it, Swedes and Norwegians bound by a blood oath. It's the biggest secret society in town."

One more Klobuchar lutefisk column. He describes how Dennis Green, coach of the Minnesota Vikings, was cornered at a football clinic by "The Norwegian," who was pushing the charms of lutefisk too hard on the unsuspecting coach.

"Momentarily stunned, Green sought refuge in chivalry.

"'Lutefisk. Right. I've heard of it.'"

Klobuchar then describes how Green was challenged to eat lutefisk. Green consulted with Klobuchar, who "told Green there were limits to how far a football coach had to go to prove to the public that he's willing to risk body and soul.

"Green said he could take as much reasonable punishment as the next guy.

"I told him lutefisk was not about reasonable punishment.

"'But you know I'm nuts about fishing. I like bass. I like walleye. I like trout. A guy wants to be polite, right?'

"Lutefisk, I said, does not belong in the same league as recognizable fish. I told him lutefisk could not be classified in any known food group and might, in fact, come closer to qualifying as a battery additive."

Only the sages of the ages can summarize such a chapter as this. On one hand there are those who like lutefisk humor because it is one big put-down. Sometimes funny, always negative. Therefore, a quotation from Mark Twain applies to this put-down group: "The secret source of Humor is not joy but sorrow." There are those who believe sorrow is the source of lutefisk—and its only reward.

On the other hand, staunch lutefisk defenders seethe at these constant knocks. They stand with Jonathan Swift when he said: "For he abhorred that senseless tribe/Who call it humor when they gibe."

Alas, most of us are in the middle. We like a good-natured laugh at lutefisk because, once in a while, we like a good-natured laugh at ourselves. It keeps us loose, lets off steam. It nudges us closer to humility and closer to each other.

8

North Dakota Notes, South Dakota Silage

These prairie people fill wide open spaces with letters, laughs, and lutefisk.

I have just one regret in writing this book: While doing my research, I could not make it to any of the lutefisk dinners in North Dakota.

My roots, on my mom's side, are in North Dakota. Darlene Schumacher, Mom, grew up as Darlene Gehring in Washburn, N.D., north of Bismarck on the banks of the Missouri River. Grandpa, Emanuel Gehring, farmed a section of wheat there. Grandma, Elsie Gehring, now 87, still lives in her house in Washburn, one block away from the First Lutheran Church. (Yes, the church does host a lutefisk dinner the last Sunday in October.) My uncle, Bill Gehring, is a physician across the river in Hazen. When I go to the Norsk Høstfest in Minot, I stay with Bill, his wife, Gloria, and their daughter, Ashley.

North Dakota represents the German side of my family. Lutefisk is not really them. Some of these folks like it, while others are tempted to belittle lutefisk. They refrain, however, because they know they would have to defend sauerkraut.

So, one of my tap roots sinks into the Peace Garden

State, and I wish I would have taken in a good old Nodak lutefisk dinner. Three times I arranged to meet Gladys Hendrickson for lutefisk at the Sons of Norway building in Fargo. Each time the plans fell through because of weather or a conflict at my end. Gladys, the first woman elected president of the Kringen 25 lodge, had even pointed out a reason to stuff myself worry-free at her table: Lutefisk won't make you fat, she said, "how can it? Every calorie has been killed."

The good news is some of the good folks of North Dakota did get their two-cents worth in this book. Gladys' daughter, Dawn Morgan, of Fargo, put together the North Dakota and northern Minnesota sections of The Lutefisk Dinner Directory. Dawn sent out news releases to local newspapers, saying she was looking for dinners to list in the directory and for amusing lutefisk tales. She got a great response, and this chapter features the highlights.

Myrna D. Lyng of Mayville, N.D., said that her husband, Merwin, helps with preparation and clean-up for the Mjosen 78 lodge lutefisk dinner. "One year he noted that the city garbage truck was parked beside the building. 'I wonder if they are picking up or delivering?' he asked."

Duane Lyng of Clifford, N.D., wrote: "Nearly 43 years ago I married a fantastic young lady who is one-half German and one-half Norwegian. I expected to get sauerkraut with my lutefisk, but she will not do that to sauerkraut."

Somehow the word spread all the way to Eric Pederson in Aberdeen, S.D., that we were looking for lutefisk stories. He wrote: "We used to save the leftover pieces of lutefisk, insert popsicle sticks into them, and freeze them. The results were known as Lute-a-Lick."

How the Irish Created Lutefisk

Richard M. Peterson said he wrote this story in his newspaper column called "Poor Richard's Almanac." The March 17, 1966, column, which ran in the *Benson County Farmers Press* in Minnewaukan, N.D., says this:

"What we celebrate on March 17 is the commemoration of St. Patrick's great and noble deed in driving the Norwegians out of Ireland. It seems that centuries ago many Norwegians came to Ireland to escape the bitterness of the Norwegian winter.

"Ireland was having a famine at the time, and food was quite scarce. The Norwegians were eating almost all the fish caught in the area, leaving the Irish with nothing but potatoes.

"St. Patrick was fearful that eventually the Norwegians would even eat the potatoes, and as a matter of fact, they were using large quantities of potatoes to make lefse.

"St. Patrick, taking matters in his own hands like most

Irishmen do, decided the Norwegians had to go. Secretly, he organized the IRATRION (Irish Republican Army To Rid Ireland Of Norwegians).

"Their first attempt failed. All through Ireland members of the IRATRION sabotaged power plants in hopes the fish in Norwegian refrigerators would spoil, forcing the Norwegians to a colder climate where their fish would keep. The fish spoiled all right, but the Norwegians, as everyone knows today, thrive on spoiled fish.

"The second attempt also met with failure. In hopes of poisoning the Norwegian intruders, members of IRATRION went into each Norwegian cave in the dead of night and sprinkled lye on the rotten fish. As everyone knows, this is how lutefisk was introduced to the Norwegians, and they thrived on this lye-soaked, stinking, spoiling fish.

"Poor St. Pat was at his wits' end as to how to get rid of the Norwegians, so he told them to go to hell!

"Sure enough, it worked! All the Norwegians left Ireland and moved to Minnesota."

Don't Do That to Lefse

I have always felt lefse would just as soon not show up at lutefisk-and-lefse dinners. Or at least have that option. Why? People associate—even confuse—lutefisk and lefse. That's acceptable if the association is good, but often it is not. Then these people who feel offended by lutefisk also feel offended by lefse. Which means lefse—a fine, harmless food if there ever was one—becomes an accomplice to the crime, forever linked with lutefisk.

The negative association worsens when these people witness someone wrapping lutefisk in lefse. To these observers, it appears as if folks who wrap fish are trying to hide something, sneaking it under the cover of lefse. To say the least, rolling lutefisk in lefse is a questionable practice, and here are two letters that discuss this topic.

In the first letter, from Phyllis Stanley of Fargo, note the use of exclamation points in back-to-back sentences, something practically unheard of in Scandinavian epistles. "My dad poured the traditional melted butter on his lutefisk, then he proceeded to put it inside his piece of homemade lefse. He would then close it and eat it like a sandwich! He devoured it graciously, even though it was somewhat messy!"

John Bye, archivist at the Institute for Regional Studies at North Dakota State University, unearthed a front-page newspaper story from the Nov. 15, 1906, *Hatton Free Press.* The editor, W.H. Kelly, wrote about accepting an invitation to a lutefisk dinner at the Free Church. Kelly said he "had never tackled anything of this kind before, but being a brave man (having served in Uncle Sam's army), he consented to go."

Kelly described waiting for the dinner of "rare fish which we used to see piled up in front of grocery stores like shocks of corn." When the other hungry diners finally sat down, Kelly said, they "immediately commenced to shovel out a few pounds of fish."

Kelly's friend told him to roll the lutefisk in lefse. "We got the second dish of ludefisk [Danish spelling], pitched into the rubber napkins [translation: very bad lefse] ... got rid of a couple pieces of cake and had just finished eating a nice big piece of juicy apple pie and called for our second cup of coffee so we could commence all over again. ..."

Read Them on the Radio

These next two letters are nice, old-fashioned letters that offer something amusing about lutefisk. They are the

 *Lutefisk Makes*

These letters revealed that lutefisk affects North Dakotans in a funny way: It makes them cheer.

Daniel S. Lee from Gwinner, N.D., wrote that 60 years ago "when I was a high school basketball player, our pep squad had a yell that they would use when we were a little tense, and it would always loosen up the fans and players and give us new strength to carry on. The first line of the yell was intended to be 'What will you have? What will you have?' but we tried to make it sound like a Norwegian brogue—so if you say it real fast it sounds something like this!

> *Wha skuta haw? Wha skuta haw?*
> *Lutefisk and lefse*
> *Yah, Yah, Yah!*

Dallas Ellingson, Oberon, N.D., wrote about a cheer "we used when I went to a country school. Don't think we used it more than once as we got in trouble with the superintendent or teacher and were told not to use it again." The cheer:

> *Lutefisk and Lefse*
> *Ya, ya, ya.*
> *We can beat (school name)*
> *Any old time.*

Such a peppy food, lutefisk.

'Em Rah-Rah

A writer who simply identified herself as Maxine sent in this cheer from her hometown of Noonan, N.D. Maxine noted that she had "no idea how to spell tus cutta ha."

Lutefisk, lefse, tus cutta ha
Noonan High School
Rah, Rah, Rah.

A similar cheer from Carol Rudrud of Fargo:

Lutefisk and Lefse
Fattigmann and Preme
Hillsboro High School
Basketball Team!

Finally, Dorothy Heieie in Fargo, N.D., got the spelling and the translation right in this basketball cheer used at Brooten High School in Brooten, Minn., in the 1940s and '50s.

Lutefisk og Lefse,
Hva skal vi ha?
   (Translation: 'What shall we have?')
A basket, a basket
Ja, ja, ja.

type of letters Garrison Keillor might read on the radio. In fact, Keillor does talk about lutefisk in his book *Lake Wobegon Days*. Here's his passage about Christmas in Lake Wobegon:

"And tubs of lutefisk appear at Ralph's meat counter, the dried cod soaked in lye solution for weeks to make a pale gelatinous substance beloved by all Norwegians, who nonetheless eat it only once a year. The soaking is done in a shed behind the store, and Ralph has a separate set of lutefisk clothes he keeps in the trunk of his Ford Galaxie. No dogs chase his car, but if he forgets to change his lutefisk socks, his wife barks at him. Ralph feels that the dish is a great delicacy, and he doesn't find lutefisk jokes funny. 'Don't knock it if you haven't tried it,' he says. Nevertheless, he doesn't offer it to the carolers who come by his house, because he knows it could kill them. You have to be ready for lutefisk.

"Father Emil doesn't knock lutefisk; he thinks it may be the Lutheran penance, a form of self-denial. His homily the Sunday before: We believe that we don't really know what's best for us, so we give up some things we like in the hope that something better might come. ..."

Jo Ann Kana of Fargo wrote about her family almost giving up lutefisk. She had struggled to carry on the tradition of Christmas Eve lutefisk dinner, "although I am the only one in our family who likes it." Every year at the meal, she had to hear "griping about lutefisk and watch everyone pass it under the table to one another." She tried to coax her family to have a bite. The reply, in unison: "'Oh, yuck!'"

So one year Jo Ann decided to stop fighting city hall: She dropped lutefisk from the holiday menu. "I thought everyone would be happy. When the food was passed I heard, 'Where's the lutefisk?' I informed them I was tired of hearing them carry on about it. [The] answer to that was a chorus of voices saying, 'But, Mom, that's a tradition!' Needless to say, the griping is back along with the lutefisk."

From Fergus Falls, Minn., on the border of North Dakota, Allan Anderson wrote this story. "One cold Saturday evening, my wife and I drove out in the countryside to a small, white wooden Lutheran church in the extreme reaches of Lyon County, Minnesota." They bought their lutefisk meal tickets, waited 30 minutes, and ate. As they were leaving, "on impulse, I asked if perhaps there was enough available to buy a plate of lutefisk which could be prepared for take-out for my mother, who was in a nursing home only 10 miles away.

"Well, this tale of filial devotion touched the hearts of the kitchen crew, and they prepared *two* servings of lutefisk. … In getting into the car, I spilled some of the juice on my new wool winter coat—my *only* winter coat! Needless to say, the smell didn't evaporate, and it wasn't until several weeks later, when the weather warmed up enough, that I could finally get the coat cleaned."

Anderson arrived at the nursing home at 9:15 p.m. and "smuggled the contraband right past" the nurses, who "probably smelled something a little strange." The lights were off in his mother's room, but she was awake. Why the surprise visit, she asked. He unveiled the lutefisk dinner for two.

The roommate, "a wonderful old Norwegian lady," was thrilled—the lutefisk came from her church. She "complained that it was a little cold, but kept wolfing it down. It also could have used some more butter—but she kept eating it, down to the last morsel! I heard from the grapevine that our odoriferous visit was the main topic of conversation around the nursing home for days."

Wanna Yob?

I end this North Dakota section with two odd notes I could not lump with anything else. Olga Hanson of Columbus, N.D., must have been in a tell-all mood when she submitted her secret beauty tip: "Lutefisk juice restores youthful appearance to skin [too much probably removes skin]. Keeps hands soft and beautiful. Used by the Venus de Milo for years." Hanson also suggested using lutefisk to eliminate tobacco breath and "slick down unruly cowlicks." (I can imagine this bumper sticker: Cowlicks? Lick 'em With Lutefisk.)

I save the oddest for last. Mary Ellen Mitchell of Bismarck submitted this job posting (which I have shortened) and apologized for not knowing who gets credit. "It is one of those things that gets passed around," she wrote. I wonder if this could be the product of a state employee with a bit too much time on his or her hands.

STATE OF NORTH DAKOTA
DEPARTMENT OF CONSUMER AFFAIRS
JOB OPPORTUNITY: Lutefisk Inspector II
SALARY RANGE: $1,295–$1,850 annually

The State of North Dakota is seeking to establish a list of persons who qualify for the position of Lutefisk Inspector II. This is not an entry level position. It requires experience and/or education. Please check all that are appropriate.

First Name: Sven _____   Last Name:_____sen/son
              Ole _____
              Lars _____

Spell LUTEFISK in the blank:
    1st Try:_____   2nd Try_____

Highest Grade Completed (Circle One): 1 2 3 4 5 6

Number of Years Required to Complete: _____

Qualified to Operate Equipment:

Fork Lift____	Fork____	Flush Toilet____
Pencil____	Doorbell____	Doormat____
Garbage Can____	Kleenex____	Bait Caster____
Snoose Can____	Bed____	Slot Machine____

List Foreign Language Proficiency:

English____	Minnesotan____	Norski____	Uff Da____
Ya Sure____	Heyya____	Svede____	Foul____

If you claim previous experience in consumption of lutefisk, show date and hospital at which you were treated:

_____

In your own words (at least three in one language) state why you want this position:

_____

NORTH DAKOTA IS AN EQUAL OPPORTUNITY EMPLOYER

- -

South Dakota Shindig

Sioux Falls, S.D., is four hours southwest of Minneapolis, but a world away. Minnesota is in the Midwest, and South Dakota is the beginning of the West. Go to a lutefisk dinner and the apparel includes cowboy hats, shirts, boots, and

A sign in the Nordic Hall basement in Sioux Falls, S.D.

Still serving in Sioux Falls, S.D.
Gladys Lovro, 82 (top), is happy to bring loaded bowls
to diners attending the Norse Glee Club's lutefisk dinner.
Joyce Farr (bottom) is also there scooping out "silage,"
which is cole slaw to most of us.

cowgirl dresses. The men have sun-baked faces with deep lines of laughter around the eyes.

I attended a lutefisk feed hosted by the Norse Glee Club in Sioux Falls. In the kitchen in the Nordic Hall basement, I watched the hustling volunteers trying to keep up with the Friday night lutefisk eaters. Gertrude Nearman organized the kitchen crew and introduced me around. I met Gladys Lovro, 82, as she picked up a dish of meatballs and scooted out into the dining hall. Gertrude introduced Joyce Farr, who was serving "silage."

"Silage?" I knew it was a dumb question, but I bit.

"You probably call it cole slaw," she said as she scooped the watery, green "silage" out of a big, plastic garbage container.

"It doesn't taste the same as it looks," said Bob Tidemann, who was nearby, dishing out meatballs. "I'm Swedish, so I do meatballs."

Glee in Nordic Hall.
Bob Tidemann serves Swedish meatballs.

Wally Wallenberg and Bob Amend called themselves the "Spudettes." One of the Spudettes (I could not keep them straight) asked about my lefse book, and then added, "You're lucky you got out alive by not writing about lutefisk first."

I took a picture of the lutefisk cook, Dick Lone, and my camera ran out of film. As I was changing rolls, he said, "You better not take out that film back here—it won't develop."

I made my way to the dining hall entryway, talking briefly with Peder Ecker, a big, friendly man, who for 25 years was a U.S. bankruptcy federal judge. "I never miss a lutefisk dinner," he said. "My grandpa used to saw the dried stockfish, and I'd hold my hands underneath to catch the sawdust. Then I'd eat it. This was in Sioux City and Sioux Falls in the 1930s."

Before stepping into the dining room for his lutefisk, Ecker wrote this poem on a piece of yellow paper and taped it on the doorway. The poem, he said, was on the wrapper of a soap for lutefisk lovers.

If you really love your lutefisk
And eat it with your fingers,
Strong soap removes the evidence
And just the memory lingers.

Rodney McClure commented that this lutefisk dinner brings friends together. "That's why I come," he said. "That and to say a few Norwegian phrases like *takk* [thanks] and *ha det bra* [literally have it good, but it is often used as a see-ya phrase]."

McClure mentioned that his grandmother had three husbands die on her. "Too much lutefisk," he said, smiling. I was not sure if he felt the grandfathers had eaten too much or that his grandmother had eaten too much, which increased her longevity.

A comedian for president.
Bob Johnson, left, and Marvin Nelson. Bob is really
Uncle Torvald, who suspended his presidential campaign
long enough to sell lutefisk tickets in Sioux Falls.

Selling tickets at the door were Bob Johnson and Marvin Nelson. I quickly surmised that these two guys were the warm-up act, something to get the people in the mood .

I had a moment to talk with Bob, who wore a "Think Lutefisk" button on his sports coat lapel. He told me he was really "Uncle Torvald," the comedian. He handed me a flyer announcing "Uncle Torvald for President." One of his campaign slogans: Put a Norwegian in the White House. You could do worse (and you usually have).

Bob explained why this Uncle Torvald name was so familiar to me. He had been Red Stangland's sidekick when they did their stand-up comedy. Stangland, the author of all those joke books, had recently died. "I miss Red," said Bob. "We did our last show on Syttende Mai in Petersburg, Alaska. We were a good act. He was the straight man, and I was the dope."

It was time for me to eat lutefisk, and I wondered what kind of Scandinavian humor I would find at the table. I sat next to Kurt Wiese, of White, S.D., and across from Jim Lusk, of Brookings, S.D. Neither one of them were Scandinavian, they said, and both were pretty sedate during the meal itself. Afterward, however, the lutefisk kicked in.

I asked Kurt how far White was from Sioux Falls. "Oh, it's about a 60-mile ride," he said with a straight face, "but it's a 100 miles with a Norwegian."

Jim, who ran a business of paying cash for old toys, seemed in a playful mood now that his blood level of lye had been elevated. He leaned over the table and said, "Watch your footing in here, Kurt. All the butter and Copenhagen [snuff] makes the floor pretty slick."

It was good fun, the kind of chuckles that shortened that dark drive back to Minneapolis that night.

At the end of the evening as I was leaving, Bob Johnson passed along this thought: "I tell people that if you go to a lutefisk supper, it's as good as taking flu shots. You'll be fine all winter."

9

Here's to the Old Ones

They keep lutefisk alive.

Lutefisk leads us back. Like many ethnic entrees, it is a peculiar food that, for an evening, yanks us out of the American melting pot and punches a hyphen back into our psyches. We remember, yes, we are Norwegian-Americans or Swedish-Americans or Danish-Americans. We are part of a line that goes back to the old country. Lutefisk helps us remember the faces in that line. We studied them as they ate the fish.

I wish I could say I had a wealth of lutefisk memories from my early years, rich connections back to holiday gatherings and an elder or two. I just don't. I'm a Gary-come-lately to lutefisk, I suppose. I waited until I was in my 40s to develop a liking for it. Some might call this my version of a mid-life crisis.

I have talked to lots of people about lutefisk, and they often tell about a loved one who has passed on, someone in their line of elders. They miss them, and lutefisk reminds them of their loss. The reminders, however, are not of a morose and moping nature. Just the opposite. They are full of mirth and warmth—the kind of memories you hear about and wish you could have been there. Worse things could be said about a food (and, with lutefisk, they have been said).

My few reminders of elders and lutefisk go back to Mom, Dad, and Uncle Cliff. All three have died in the last year. The reminders floated around me at three lutefisk dinners: one in Madison, Wis.; one put on by the Norwegian Glee Club in Minneapolis; and one two blocks away from my home at Mount Olivet Lutheran Church in Minneapolis.

Sweet Music in Madison

After a lutefisk dinner at the Norway Center in Madison, I hung around with members of the Dane County Grieg Male Chorus. The lutefisk and the meal had been fine, but nothing could be finer than their singing. This was not re-hearsed—these guys would just break out in some song as if they could not help themselves. Sun comes up, birds gotta sing. Grieg chorus gathers, guys gotta sing. They only sang twice, but each time it was clearly for my benefit. I do not overstate it when I say I felt embraced by song and by heritage. And, thanks to one chorus member, I found myself thinking about fishing with Uncle Cliff.

The first time they sang, everyone was in the kitchen having a Miller as they prepared the meal. Jon Gullixson and Gary Hendrickson were cooking the lutefisk, both of them students of John and Sophie Refvik. John Refvik had passed on, but Sophie was there looking over the boys' shoulders. All of a sudden, a boisterous song, well sung, erupted around the stainless-steel kitchen table: *"Helen går, sjung hopp-fal-le-ral-la lej ..."* they sang. As the song ended, beer cans went up and the contents went down. The title was *"Helen Går"* and the message was clear: bottoms up. Drink in the whole thing.

After the meal and clean-up, Jon Grinde gave me a tour

of the basement bottle locker room. The basement was large, dark, dank, cold, and cluttered with food boxes and empty plastic lutefisk containers. We went into a small room lit by two bare bulbs. A couple of old tables with chairs sat to the side. On one wall hung three rows of small wooden lockers, each with a lock and each large enough to hold a liquor bottle. I did not ask, but I assumed chorus members over the years used the lockers to store their favorite brand of whiskey or *aquavit*. What gave me pause was the feeling that Jon was showing me a hideaway, that locked heritage doors were opening and a club that included my elders had accepted me.

The second song, sung when Jon and I returned upstairs at the Norway Center, was *"Aftensolen,"* which means "The Evening Sun." A tender song for when the day is done. One of the men singing was Alvar Nyberg, a

Harmonious heritage.
Alvar Nyberg, 88, has been singing second tenor with the Dane County Grieg Male Chorus for 66 years.

Swedish-American who had been singing second tenor for 66 years. He was approaching his 88th birthday.

Alvar reminded me of my uncle Clifford Bengtson, who had also been Swedish-American. He was 82 when he died at home in Richfield, Minn. He often took on the role of a father to me. The last few years, when he and his four grown boys and I would take August fishing trips to northern Minnesota and Wisconsin, Cliff and I would usually end up together in a boat on the lake, quietly catching weeds. One time, though, I caught a nice-sized largemouth bass—which was good. But I had used Cliff's lure—which was bad, because of all the kidding I took from him over

Fishing and lutefisk. Clifford Bengtson, my lutefisk uncle. "Well, we didn't do much today, but we'll go get 'em tomorrow."

the years. Whenever I'd brag about that fish he'd jokingly remind me that there would be no story without his lure. "Just what were you using when you caught that bass, Gary?" he'd ask rhetorically.

In a way, I returned the favor to Cliff because I was with him when he caught his last fish. We paddled out on the lake in a canoe one evening after a rain, and he hooked a "snake," a small northern pike. He put it back, and we went ashore. The day ended with his standard summary: "Well, we didn't do much today, but we'll go get 'em tomorrow."

Cliff was my lutefisk uncle. For about the last eight years of his life, my Christmas gift to him and Aunt Benora was a lutefisk dinner at King Oscar's in Richfield. One of their sons, Darroll, usually came along. So did Cliff's granddaughter, Kim Venuta, and her husband, Pete Venuta. Pete popped a few eyeballs the year he joined us. When the lutefisk was served, he pulled out a small bottle of Tabasco sauce. I give Pete, a man of Italian heritage, credit for even ordering lutefisk. Only about half of us at these gatherings did. Kim, my wife Jane, son Ben, and daughter Kate ordered anything but lutefisk.

I remember the first time we fed lutefisk to Kate, whom we adopted from Colombia. She was 11 months old, and we were doing our annual King Oscar's dinner. Against Jane's wishes, I put a little sliver of lutefisk on Kate's highchair tray. We all watched. She put it into her mouth and swallowed. She let out what I called her "baby rhino" grunt, which she used when she liked a food. She grunted again, and her chubby legs stiffened. "I think she likes it, Cliff," I said. She has outgrown her love of lutefisk, but I believe she will be back someday.

Cliff died of brain tumors, in his own bed, held and caressed by his family. I went to see him a couple times in his final days, when he was usually unresponsive. The night I

Here's to the old ones,
Whose next year is "no"
Or "maybe," at best.
They come, slowly, for lutefisk,
Nicked up by time,
Carrying humility like a handbag,
Tipping the hat to death.

They come for the fish,
Now, on the arms of the babies they once carried.

Here's to the old ones,
Who are lured by the lute, by the laughs, by the lefse.
They delight in the din, in the
Swoosh of the smell that they know oh, so well.
They sniff and are six again,
Wrinkling their noses at a stinky thing soaking.
"You really gonna eat that, Grandpa Sven?"

Here's to the old ones.
While we wander in our youth far from home,
They keep these grand dinners alive.
They are elms, serving shade, holding firm, staying put.
They are windbreaks at odds with erosion.

Old Ones

When they tire of squinting at gales in their faces
They cry, but then joke about fish.

They come to sup, to "yup," to
Link arms with their old ones.
They wait in red-padded pews,
Toes tapping, hands cupped over canes,
Backs bent, chins high, hair coiffed up and ruled.
Foreheads spit-shined by scrubbing.
They lean into lutefisk, full forks raising eyebrows.

Tonight, for a night, they are towers once more.
They walk from the church rather sprightly.
On front porches you hear
The tic of a cane? Nope.
The toc of life's clock? Yes.

When I become old,
Will my kids carry me?
Will I whistle down parkways
At age 93?
I wonder:
Will lutefisk continue to be?
Yessireeee!

took my family to say farewell, one of Cliff's sons, Steve, was there holding Cliff's hand. I sat with them for quite a while, not saying much. Jane was talking with Benora and Darroll in the front room. Finally, it was time to go. I figured this was probably the last time I would see Cliff alive, but I did not want to say good-bye. So I grabbed his hand and said, "Gotta go, Cliff. Next time I'll bring you some lutefisk." I would like to believe I saw his lips part, as if to smile.

A Surprise Greeting From Mom

Mom was not a lutefisk lady. Darlene Gehring was German-American, and she married my dad, Conrad Legwold, a Norwegian-American. When I was an infant, they occasionally visited my dad's parents, Jennie and Carl Legwold, in Peterson, Minn., at Christmastime. Lutefisk was served, but Mom was far less fond of lutefisk than she was of Grandma Legwold. Grandma was one of those all-accepting saints, tall and strong. From her pantry emerged miracle treats, such as lefse. (She was the one who inspired me to make lefse and write my first book.) The pantry was also where Grandma kept the peppermint schnapps. One Christmas, Mom arrived with menstrual cramps, and Grandma suggested that she take a little sip of schnapps to ease the pain.

So other than the schnapps memory, I do not think of lutefisk when I think of Mom. However, about six weeks after she died suddenly of a heart attack, her name came up at a lutefisk dinner at the Lutheran Church of the Good Shepherd in Minneapolis. The Norwegian Glee Club of Minneapolis hosted the dinner. I was there with Jane; Bitten Norvoll, one of the lefse makers featured in my lefse book; and Odd and Randi Unstad, the Norwegians who taught me to make lutefisk.

We all were seated for lutefisk. The Glee Club sang at this dinner, and a singing accordion player roamed the room. Then from the kitchen came Florence Henderson. "I knew your Mom, Gary," she said.

"You're the one I talked with on the phone," I replied, and I shook her hand. Florence had called one day about

Darlene Schumacher.
A remembrance of Mom in her young, working-woman days came up at the lutefisk dinner hosted by the Norwegian Glee Club of Minneapolis.

arrangements for the cover photo of this book, which was to be shot at the Glee Club dinner. She also had asked about Mom. It turned out that Florence and Mom had roomed together as young women working in Minneapolis. Mom had worked for Western Union in the Foshay Tower. We talked about the details of her death, and she expressed her sympathy. She also asked about Dad. I told her he had died a year earlier.

After a short while talking at the table, Florence went back to preparing the lutefisk meal, and I went back to eating it. But I was moved to think that a friend from Mom's big-dream days just happened to be at the same church where I was eating lutefisk. It was Mom saying, "Hi, Gar."

We finished our food and began walking out. A long line was waiting for the next seating. Odd, ever looking for a laugh, turned to me and said with a straight face—and just loud enough for those in line to hear: "Too bad they ran out of lutefisk."

This brought a few nervous chuckles from the line, and more than a few hard stares of concern. Then, to heighten concern, Odd added, "They still have the meatballs at least."

The Walk Home From Church

Mount Olivet Lutheran Church in Minneapolis is two blocks away from my house. Former Mount Olivet pastors have lived in my house. This is not where I worship, but many of my neighbors do. It is where I vote and where my daughter, Kate, went to preschool. I bike, jog, walk, or drive by it every day. My children have played soccer and baseball on fields that, on lazy spring and fall evenings, are literally in the church's shadows. Mount Olivet is a central part of my neighborhood.

When Mount Olivet has its annual lutefisk dinner the first Friday in December, the church parking lot fills up, and cars line the elm-arched streets. The question among neighbors not tuned into lutefisk happenings is: What's the big deal at the church tonight?

Everything seems like a big deal at Mount Olivet. With some 12,000 members, it is the largest Lutheran congregation in the United States, according to church records. One spring Sunday, in celebration of the church's 75th anniversary, the congregation took over the Target Center, the sports and entertainment arena in Minneapolis, for one big service instead of having morning services every hour on the hour. As for the lutefisk dinner in December, it draws around 1,800 faithful in four hours.

I have attended two of Mount Olivet's lutefisk dinners, and each time I have walked to the church. Something about that walk I really like. Something symbolic. I always see others walking to the dinner too, and it is nice knowing like-minded people live close. I feel as if I have gratefully dropped out of the drive-like-crazy world and have stepped back into sanity. It's as if for one evening in a big city, my world becomes more like a small town—slower, cozier, more contained.

Last year, I entered the church and walked back to Mount Olivet's kitchen, where Eileen Scott was running the show, trying to get the 100 volunteers organized before the 4 o'clock sitting. "One year about 10 years ago, there was a sleet storm," she said. "The lights went out and we were back here cooking by candlelight." She showed me records of Mount Olivet's first lutefisk dinner, held in the home of Mrs. Serley Feb. 23, 1929. Mrs. Bliss, Mrs. Woodfill, and Mrs. Andresen also served on the committee that organized the dinner, which raised $29.85. These days Mount Olivet dinners, said Eileen, raise about $10,000.

The volunteers were buzzing around, and I tried to record some names. Fran Swanson was taking tickets, Larry Larson was boiling potatoes, and Grace Hagen was waiting to hand out lefse at the buffet table. "That's Grace as in Kelly, and Hagen as in Copenhagen," she said with a smile. Grace said she remembered her mother making lutefisk in the kitchen and her father bringing home the stockfish on the streetcar. Later, when passing out two rolls of lefse per person, Grace was a soft touch for the common request: "Can I have another? I haven't had lefse for so long."

As people started going through the line, I went to the kitchen to say hello to the crew. "There are two things in this world I don't like: standing in line and spending money," said Jay Lansing. "And people are out there standing in line and spending money on this stuff." Nick Huble was cutting up fish, Jerry Iwen was arranging the chunks in oven pans (this crew bakes the lutefisk). He said the chunks go "green side up." I figured out from my sod-laying days as a landscaper that this meant putting the skin side down. Hazel Iwen and Warren Dahl were sliding fish in and out of the oven. Ralph Berglund and Loren Johnson were scooping hot lutefisk from the pans into serving dishes.

The line was very long now; it ran the entire length of the long dining hall and wound out toward the church door. As the evening went on, the line did not let up. It appeared that this could be a record year. I asked why this year? Someone heard that *Star Tribune* sports writer Sid Hartman, of all people, had promoted Mount Olivet's dinner that morning on WCCO radio, as did Joyce Lamont on KLBB radio.

"I don't know how we'll feed this crowd," said Eileen, looking concerned. Some of the lutefisk crew were devising

A really big show.
Warren Dahl was baking lutefisk the night Mount Olivet
Lutheran Church broke its own record: 1,900 served.

plans for slipping out the back. They would take for themselves the little lutefisk that was left, and barricade the door behind them. That was a ploy fraught with peril, I suggested, because nothing is so alarming as Lutherans denied their lutefisk. If the parishioners had discovered that someone had absconded with their lutefisk, they would have reduced this sprawling church campus to rubble.

When the evening ended, everyone, including the volunteers, was well-fed and happy. What's more, Mount Olivet had set a new record: 1,900 served.

Nick, who had cut the fish for all 1,900 servings, had red, swollen hands. "But look how this stuff shines up jewelry," he said, showing his brightened rings.

Eileen was tired, half-heartedly wondering how much longer she could do this. "I don't know, I wonder how crazy I am," she said. "But the people are so appreciative."

Not every year will be a record year, I said to comfort

Conrad Legwold.
When Dad was a boy in Peterson, Minn.,
his family ate lutefisk on Christmas Eve, then
walked a mile to the evening church service.

her. Yes, she said, the day's mild temperatures and timely snowfall had helped bring out the record crowd. "The fish man says you have to have a little snow for people to think lutefisk."

On my walk home, a dreamy snow was falling. Looking up into the street lamps, I understood that winter gives water a chance to dance. I thought of Dad and a recollection he shared with me shortly before he died. Grandma would make lutefisk on Christmas Eve, he said, and dress up as Santa Claus to present her five children with gifts. Then the family would walk to the evening church service.

Dad did not say much more than that, but I imagined Grandpa, limping with his bad knee, and Grandma leading her five children—Benora, Conrad, Lloyd, Evelyn, and Curt. The gloved hands of the big people joined the mittened hands of the little ones as they walked the mile to church. They walked on the snow-packed gravel road that wound around the bluffs and into town. Some years, the nights were cold and the moon was high. I could imagine the silhouette of those seven, walking by moonlight. Other years, to be sure, the night must have been just like tonight—mild enough so you felt no need to scrunch up your shoulders and lower your head to the wind. You could stand outside the church for a moment, watching the snow fall in the rose-stained glow from the windows.

The Lutefisk Dinner Directory

ALASKA
Anchorage
Bernt Balchen 46,
  Sons of Norway
Viking Hall
8141 Briarwood St.
Anchorage, AK 99518
Friday and Saturday before
  Thanksgiving, 5–8 p.m.
Tickets $17.50, reservations
  encouraged, 907-349-1613
Serves 200
Note: They use red snapper for
  their lutefisk and bake it.

Fairbanks
Sons of Norway
Fairbanks Lutheran Church
1012 Cowles St.
Fairbanks, AK 99701
Usually second Sunday in
  October, 4–6 p.m.
Tickets at door, $15 adults, $7.50
  children 6-12, under 6 free
Serves 100

Homer
Faith Lutheran Church
2634 Soundview Ave.
Homer, AK 99603
907-235-7600
Second weekend in November,
  usually 7 p.m.

Tickets $10, call the church or
  Turc Olson at 907-235-5107
Serves 150
Note: People dress in costume.
  Turc and his wife, Lorna tell
  lots of Ole and Lena jokes.

Juneau
Sons of Norway
Juneau Yacht Club
Juneau, AK 99801
David Moe, 907-789-2857
Around the Christmas Holiday
Tickets at door, $10, members
  only
Serves 120–130
Note: Christmas concert after the
  dinner.

Kodiak
Elks Lodge
102 Marine Way
Kodiak, AZ 99615
Saturday, late October or early
  November, times vary
Tickets at door, $10
Serves 200
Note: Music by local group, "Carl
  and Carl" play accordion and
  guitar.

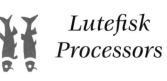

Lutefisk Processors

For information on purchasing
lutefisk or ling stockfish, contact:

Day Fish Co.
4409 409th Ave. N.W.
Braham, MN 55006
612-396-3468

Mike's Fish and Seafood, Inc.
Highway 55
Glenwood, MN 56334
1-800-950-4755

New Day Fisheries
2427 Washington St.
Port Townsend, WA 98368
360-385-4600

Olsen Fish Co.
815 North 5th St.
Minneapolis, MN 55401-1126
1-800-882-0212

Island Viking 145,
  Sons of Norway
Patrick Crittenden, 907-486-4806
Third Saturday in November,
  6 p.m.
For tickets and location, write:
  Island Viking Lodge 2-145
  PO Box 3995
  Kodiak, AK 99615-3995
Tickets $10–15 adults, less for
  children
Serves 200
Note: The lutefisk is made locally
  from cod by two lodge mem-
  bers. Music and dancing.

Palmer
Moose Lodge
1136 South Cobb
Palmer, AK 99645
907-745-4982
First Saturday in December,
  6 p.m.
Call for ticket information, $12
Serves 150–200

Petersburg
Sons of Norway Hall
23 Sing Lee Alley
Petersburg, AK 99833
907-772-4575
A Sunday in February, 5 p.m.
Call for ticket information, no
  charge for members.
Serves 100

Sitka
In January
Tickets $5, members only,
  contact Lois Rhodes,
  710 Lake St.
  Sitka, AK 99835
  907-747-3671
Serves 40
Note: The dinner is held in members homes. They rent a bus
  and go from home to home,
  each with a different course to
  eat. This enables people to
  serve alcoholic drinks without
  anyone having to drive home.

ARIZONA
Scottsdale
Desert Fjord 133, Sons of Norway
Masonic Lodge
1531 N. Scottsdale Rd.
Scottsdale, AZ 85254
602-946-1072
Second Sunday in December, 12,
  1:30, and 3 p.m.
Reservations, $12.50, write:
  Desert Fjord 133
  Sons of Norway
  PO Box 61374
  Phoenix, AZ 85082-1374
Serves 300
Note: The lutefisk is from
  Minnesota. They have dancing,
  music, and a boutique at the
  dinner.

CALIFORNIA
Denair
Garborg 56, Sons of Norway
Denair Community Center
  Lions Hall
Gratton Rd.
Denair, CA 95316
Second or third Saturday in
  November, 6 p.m. social hour,
  7 p.m. dinner
Reservations, $15, contact:
  Eric Beck
  1420 Giahos Ave.
  Modesto, CA 95358
  209-578-0927
Serves 100–150

Los Gatos
Nordahl Grieg 52,
  Sons of Norway
Nordahl Hall
580 W. Parr Ave.
Los Gatos, CA 95030
408-374-4454
First Friday and Saturday in
  December
Friday, $13.50, 5:30–9:30 p.m.
Saturday, $17.50, dinner and
  dance, 6 p.m.
Reservations required. Tickets go
  on sale November 1. Write:

JoAnne Ansok
18383 Monttere Way
Saratoga, CA 95070
Serves 1,200
Note: A bazaar is held both
nights.

Oakland
Bjornstjerne Bjornson 14,
Sons of Norway
Bjornson Hall
2258 MacArthur Blvd.
Oakland, CA 94602
510-531-9882
First Saturday in November,
5–8 p.m.
Reservations, $12–14, call Nancy
Eikeberg, 510-530-3721
Serves 250–275

Palos Verdes
Ulabrand 24, Sons of Norway
Nansen Field/
Roland Hills Estates
15 Hidden Valley Rd.
Palos Verdes, CA 90274
310-375-3377
Second or third Saturday in
November, 6:30 p.m.
Reservations, $15, contact:
Patricia Patten
6724 Los Verdes Dr., Apt. 4
Rancho Palos Verdes,
CA 90275
310-541-7250
Serves 100
Note: The lutefisk is from
Minnesota. They discuss the
legend of lutefisk, the culture,
and its humor.

Placentia
Solbakken 64, Sons of Norway
Round Table Clubhouse
901 N. Bradford Ave.
Placentia, CA 92670
714-525-9278
Third Saturday in November,
4 and 6:30 p.m.
Reservations, $13–15, contact
Jerry Patraborg
1431 Avolencia Dr.
Fullerton, CA 92635
714-871-4521
Serves 300–400

Sacramento
Roald Amundsen 48,
Sons of Norway
Sons of Norway Hall
770 Darina Ave.
Sacramento, CA 95815
916-925-9590
First Saturday in October and
fourth Saturday in March,
5–7:30 p.m.
Reservations contact:
Florence Smith
606 JoAnne Lane
Roseville, CA 95678
916-783-8830
Tickets $13.50 adults,
$5 children under 10
Serves 400–500
Note: Door prizes and dancing
after dinner.

San Diego
Valhall 25, Sons of Norway
East San Diego Masonic Temple
7849 Tommy St.
San Diego, CA 92119
Third Saturday in February,
3 and 6:30 p.m.
Reservations, $11.30, call
Jim Adams, 619-541-0676
Serves 400–600
Note: Norwegian-trained chefs
serve traditional meal with
lefse and rice sauce for dessert.
People dress in native
costumes. Swedish, Danish,
and Finnish are also welcome.

San Pablo
Andrew Furuseth 49,
Sons of Norway
Moose Lodge
13233 San Pablo Ave.
San Pablo, CA 94806
510-234-5737
Second Saturday in November,
6:30 p.m.
Reservations, $12–15, contact
Margaret Floe
601 Humboldt St.
Richmond, CA 94805-1915
510-234-5062
Serves 200
Note: Dance after dinner.

Van Nuys
Norrona 50, Sons of Norway
Sons of Norway Hall
14312 Friar St.
Van Nuys, CA 91401-2115
818-780-4778
First Friday and Saturday in
   November and last Friday and
   Saturday in January
Friday, 4:30–8 p.m. Saturday,
   4–8 p.m.
Tickets at door, $15, all you can
   eat
Serves 1,000
Note: 30–40 year tradition. They
   have a boutique selling
   Norwegian items.

Ventura
Balder 68, Sons of Norway
Trinity Lutheran Church
Ventura, CA 93003
805-644-7474
Second Saturday in November,
   5 and 6:30 p.m.
Tickets $11, write:
   Ordale Johnson
   524 LaFonda Dr.
   Ventura, CA 93003
Serves 225–300

COLORADO
Colorado Springs
Fjellheim 107, Sons of Norway
Benet Hill Center
2577 N. Chelton Rd.
Colorado Springs, CO 80909
719-473-6184
Saturday after second Wednesday
   in November, 5, 6 and 7 p.m.
Tickets $9, call Viking Hall,
   719-574-3717
Serves 600

Lakewood
Trollheim 110, Sons of Norway
Trollheim Lodge
6610 W. 14th Ave.
Lakewood, CO 80214
303-422-3394

First Saturday in November,
   6 p.m.
Reservations, $10–15, contact
   Robert Fing
   3905 Dover St.
   Wheat Ridge, CO 80033
   303-422-3394
Serves 350

FLORIDA
Jacksonville
Gateway to Florida 541,
   Sons of Norway
904-268-3457
Location changes
Second Friday in December,
   7 p.m.
Reservations, $7–10, contact
   Mary Beth Ingvoldstad
   8787 Southside Blvd. #4616
   Jacksonville, FL 32256
   904-363-6132
Serves 100

IDAHO
Boise
Grondal 122, Sons of Norway
Officers Club
Gowen Field
Boise, ID 83705
First Saturday in November,
   2–7 p.m.
Reservations, $12.50, write:
   Eleanor Stafford
   1735 N. Black Cat Rd.
   Meridian, ID 83642-5363
Serves 150

Coeur d'Alene
Harald Haarfager 11,
   Sons of Norway
Odd Fellows Hall
403 Coeur d'Alene St.
Coeur d'Alene, ID 83814
First weekend in November,
   5 and 7 p.m.
Tickets $8, contact:
   Bob Evenson
   Route 3, Box 139A
   Hayden Lake, ID 83835
   208-772-6902
Serves 70–80

Idaho Falls
Valhalla 113, Sons of Norway
Sons of Norway Hall/Riverdale
Grange Hall
New Sweden Rd.
Idaho Falls, ID 83401
Second Friday in November,
6:30 p.m.
Tickets $5, write:
Don Combs
1050 S. 168th St. E.
Victor, ID 83401
Serves 50–60

ILLINOIS
Arlington Heights
Skjold 100, Sons of Norway
Scandinavian Club
2323 N. Wilke Rd.
Arlington Heights, IL 60004
First Sunday in December,
1–3 p.m.
Reservations, call the Club,
708-870-1710
$17 adults, $6 children under 12
Serves 80–100

IOWA
Decorah
Big Canoe Lutheran Church
1381 Big Canoe Rd.
Decorah, IA 52101-7420
319-546-7978
Second Sunday in November,
4–8:30 p.m.
Tickets: Advance only. Call
church.
$8.50 adults, $3.50 children
under 12
Serves 500

Cliff House Restaurant
PO Box 49
Decorah, IA 52101
319-382-4241
Every Sunday, buffet or off of the
menu, 11 a.m.–2 p.m.
Tickets $6.95 adults,
$3.95 children under 13
Serves 400-600

Glenwood Lutheran Church
1197 Old Stage Rd.
Decorah, IA 52101
319-382-2747
First Sunday in November,
4 p.m. until all are served
Tickets at door, $8 adults, $3
children under 12
Serves 400

Luther College
700 College Dr.
Decorah, IA 52101
319-387-2000
Last Sunday in July, Nordic Fest,
11 a.m.–12:30 p.m.
Tickets at door, $8 adults, $4
children 5–10, under 5 free

VFW
104 State St,
Decorah, IA 52101
319-382-5232
Second Saturday in November
Tickets at door, $7.50 adults,
$3.50 children
Serves 200–250

Forest City
Waldorf College
106 S. Sixth St.
Forest City, IA 50436
515-582-2450
First weekend in December,
Saturday, 6 p.m., Sunday, 5 p.m.
Tickets in advance, $12 buffet
style, contact the college
Serves 248 each night
Note: Dinners are candlelit, and
they serve roast pork, meatballs, and lutefisk. The dinner
includes Christmas concert,
dinner, and a reception at the
president's house.

Jericho
*Crane Creek Emmanuel
Lutheran Church*
Bethany Hall
First or second Sunday in
October, evening
Tickets in advance, contact:
Merlin Heimerdinger
20675 Robin Ave.
Lawler, IA 52154
319-569-8549

$8 adults, $5 children over 5,
    under 5 free
Serves 300–350

Northwood
First Lutheran Church
309 Ninth St. N.
Northwood, IA 50459
515-324-2984
Second Sunday in November,
    time varies
Tickets $10 adults, $5 children,
    contact church
Serves 240

Osage
Rock Creek Lutheran Church
3269 Foothill Ave.
Osage, IA 50461
515-732-4270
Fourth Thursday in October,
    time varies
Tickets in advance, $9 adults,
    $4.50 children, contact church
Serves 400

Rake
Rake Community School
Rake, IA 50465
515-562-2979
Last Saturday in February,
    3–7 p.m.
Tickets at door, $8 adults, $3.50
    children
Serves 500–700

Sioux City
*Sons of Norway Glitne Sioux
    Viking 167 and
    Nordic Male Chorus*
Scandinavian Society Building
1801 Fourth St.
Sioux City, IA 51101
Early November, time varies
Tickets at door and in advance,
    $6.50 adults, $3.50 children
    under 10. Call Willis Hanson,
    712-276-1131
Serves 300–400

Story City
*Kong Sverre 482,
    Sons of Norway*
Sons of Norway Hall
503 Elm Ave.
Story City, IA 50248
515-733-4656
Late October, 4–7 p.m.
Tickets at door and in advance,
    $8 adults, $4 children under 12
Note: They serve cod that is
    dipped in batter, fried, and
    then held in steam table.

MARYLAND
Timonium
Norwegian American Club
Holiday Inn
2004 Green Spring Dr.
Timonium, MD 21093
Third Wednesday in December,
    7:30 p.m.
Reservations, $25, call
    Norwegian American Club,
    410-252-7373
Serves 75
Note: The Norwegian National
    Anthem is sung before dinner.
    After dinner they sing Christ-
    mas carols and dance.

MICHIGAN
Farmington
Swedish Club
Finnish Center Association
West Eight-Mile Rd.
Farmington, MI
810-478-2563
Sunday after second Friday in
    December, 2 p.m.
Tickets $15
Serves 200–250

MINNESOTA
Adams
Little Cedar Lutheran Church
3078 Lewiston St. NW
Adams, MN 55909
507-582-3185
First Wednesday in November,
    11a.m.–1:30 p.m.
    and 4:30–8 p.m.
Tickets at door, $9–$10
Serves 1,200

Alexandria
Calvary Lutheran Church
605 Douglas
Alexandria, MN 56308
612-763-5178
Last Friday in January, 4–8 p.m.
Tickets at door, $8 adults, $4.50
  ages 7–16, under 6 free
Serves 700–800

Anoka
Zion Lutheran Church
1601 Fourth Ave. S.
Anoka, MN 55303-2491
612-421-4656
First Monday in December,
  4, 5:30 and 7 p.m.
Tickets $8, call church in mid-
  November to reserve
Serves 900
Note: They have had the dinner
  for 35 years.

Aurora
Our Savior's Lutheran Church
302 S. Second Ave. E
Aurora, MN 55705
218-229-3214
First Thursday in November,
  4–7 p.m.
Tickets at door, usually $7.50,
  call church to reserve
Serves 250
Note: Cartoons about lutefisk are
  posted.

Badger
Faith Lutheran Church
Badger, MN 56714
218-528-3231
In October, 5–8 p.m.
Tickets $6
Serves 200

Barnesville
Our Savior's Lutheran Church
302 Third St. NE
Barnesville, MN 56514
218-354-7101
Last Sunday in October,
  12–5 p.m.
Tickets $8.50
Serves 500–600

Baudette
First Lutheran Church
312 Third Ave. S.W.
Baudette, MN 56623
218-634-1744
First Sunday in November,
  3–7 p.m.
Tickets $8
Serves 250

Bemidji
Calvary Lutheran Church
2508 Washington Ave. S.
Bemidji, MN 56601
218-751-1884
Last Thursday in November,
  5–7 p.m.
Tickets $7.50 advance or at door
Serves 300

Eagle's Club
1270 Neilson St.
Bemidji, MN 56601
218-751-9985
Mid-November, 6:30–8 p.m.
Tickets at door, $7.50
Serves 150

Blooming Prairie
First Lutheran Church
434 First St. SW
Blooming Prairie, MN
  55917-0697
507-583-6621
Third Tuesday in October,
  11 a.m.–1 p.m. and 4–8 p.m.
Tickets $10, call church starting
  October 1 to reserve
Serves 2,200
Note: Women who serve are
  dressed in traditional
  Norwegian costumes.

Bock
Kountry Kettle Restaurant
1683 Wall St.
Bock, MN 56313
612-556-3531
Mid-November through January,
  4:30–9 p.m.
Tickets $8, buffet style
Serves 75 at a time.

Brooklyn Center
Cross of Glory Lutheran Church
5929 Brooklyn Blvd.
Brooklyn Center, MN 55429
612-533-8602
October, time varies, but usually
3 seatings
Tickets $10, presale starts first of
October
Serves 360

Byron
East St. Olaf
6200 County Rd. 3 SW
Byron, MN 55920
507-365-8222
First Friday in November,
11 a.m.–1 p.m. and 4–8 p.m.
Tickets $9, noon serving at door,
evening in advance
Serves 1,500

Cambridge
Cambridge Lutheran Church
Fellowship Hall
621 N. Old Main St.
Cambridge, MN 55008
612-689-1211
First Thursday in November,
3–7 p.m.
Tickets $8, reservations
encouraged
Serves 900

Cannon Falls
Edgewood Restaurant
7860 365th St. Way
7 miles south of Cannon Falls on
Hwy 52
Cannon Falls, MN 55009-5226
507-263-5700
Mondays September through
December, 5–10 p.m.
$11.50, reservations
recommended, buffet

Cloquet
Hope Lutheran Church
4093 Munger Shaw Rd.
Munger, MN 55720
218-729-6380
First Sunday in December,
4–7 p.m.
Tickets at door or call church in
advance, cost varies

Serves 150–200
Note: Money goes toward a
different mission each year.

Our Savior's Lutheran Church
12th Street and
Doddridge Avenue
Cloquet, MN 55720
218-879-1535
First Wednesday in December,
4:30–7 p.m.
Tickets at door, $8
Serves 250

Columbia Heights
*First Lutheran Church of
Columbia Heights*
1555 40th Ave. NE
Columbia Heights, MN
55421-3103
612-572-8297
Second Saturday in January,
12, 2, 4, and 6 p.m.
Tickets required, $10, contact
church starting in mid-December.
Serves 1,000

Crystal
St. James Lutheran Church
6700 46th Place N.
Crystal, MN 55428-5199
612-537-3653
Third Saturday in November,
5 and 6 p.m.
Tickets $10, call church for reser-
vations
Serves 220

Dennison
Vang Lutheran Church
PO Box 117
Dennison, MN 55018
507-789-5186
Second Wednesday in October,
11 a.m., 12, and 1 p.m. Open
seating from 4–8 p.m.
Tickets $10, reservations re-
quested starting in September,
507-789-5350, 645-5084, or
263-5634.

Duluth
First Lutheran Church
1110 E. Superior St.
Duluth, MN 55802
218-728-3668

Late November or early
   December, 5–7:30 p.m. and
   lunch times vary
Tickets in advance or at door,
   $7.50–10
Serves 300–500

East Bethel
Our Savior's Lutheran Church
1562 Viking Blvd. NE
East Bethel, MN 55011
Larry, 612-753-4453
October, 5–7 p.m.
Tickets $8 adults, $4 children
   under 12, advance recom-
   mended, contact church

Emmons
Emmons Lutheran Church
490 Pearl St.
Emmons, MN 56029
507-297-5471
Second Tuesday in November,
   12, 5, 6, 7 and 8 p.m.
Tickets $9.50 adults, less for chil-
   dren, reservations
   required. Contact First State
   Bank, 507-297-5461 or Beth
   507-297-5842.
Serves 1,000

Faribault
Lavender Inn
2424 Lyndale
Faribault, MN 55021
First Thursday in November,
   11:30 a.m.–8 p.m.
Tickets at door or advance, $9,
   contact First English Lutheran
   Church, 507-334-4389
204 Second St. NW
Faribault, MN 55021
Serves 700–750
Note: Servers are dressed in
   Norwegian costume.

Fairmont
Grace Lutheran Church
300 South Grant St.
Fairmont, MN 56031
507-238-4418
November, 4–7 p.m.
Tickets at door or advance,
   $8–$10

Serves 300–350
Note: Cooks and servers dress in
   Norwegian costume.

Farmington
Highview Christiania Church
26690 Highview Ave. W
Farmington, MN 55024-9236
612-469-2722
First Saturday in October,
   3:30–7:30 p.m.
Tickets $9 adults, $4.50 children
   under 11, reservations
   required
Serves 300

Flom
Aspland Lutheran Church
Flom, MN 56541
218-584-8686
First Sunday in November,
   4–6:30 p.m.
Tickets $7
Serves 200

Forest Lake
Faith Lutheran Church
886 North Shore Dr.
Forest Lake, MN 55025-1299
612-464-3323
First Tuesday of December,
   4:30–7 p.m.
Tickets at door, $8
Serves 650

Fridley
Redeemer Lutheran Church
Activities Center
61 Mississippi Way NE
Fridley, MN 55432
Marion, 612-757-1256
A Thursday in October, 4–7 p.m.
Tickets $8, in advance starting
   3 weeks before dinner
Serves 375
Note: A woman plays piano, and
   a man plays guitar. Homemade
   lefse is sold. Greeting cards
   and napkins on sale too.

Frost
Dell Church
Route 1, Box 11
Frost, MN 56033
507-878-3391

First Sunday in February,
1–6 p.m.
Tickets at door or advance, $8.50
Note: Dining area is decorated in
Norwegian memorabilia.

Gatzke
Our Savior's Lutheran Church
At Thief Lake
Gatzke, MN 56724
218-459-3314
Last Saturday in October, 4 and
8:30 p.m.
Tickets $6
Serves 250

Glenwood
Glenwood Retirement Village
719 SE Second St.
Glenwood, MN 56334
612-634-5131
First Wednesday in November,
4:30–8 p.m.
Tickets at door, $6.50
Serves 450–500
Note: They call it the "Lutefisk
Holiday."

Goodridge
Faith Lutheran Church
Vaughn St.
Goodridge, MN 56725
218-378-4638
Second Sunday in October,
4:30–8 p.m.
Tickets $8
Serves 450–500

Grand Meadow
Grand Meadow Lutheran Church
115 First St. NW
Grand Meadow, MN 55936
507-754-5203
First Sunday in October,
11 a.m.–7 p.m.
Tickets at door or advance, $9,
call 2 weeks in advance.
Serves 400–500
Note: This will be their second
year.

Grand Rapids
Zion Lutheran Church
2901 S. Highway 169
Grand Rapids, MN 55744
218-326-8553

First Saturday in December, all
afternoon
Tickets at door, cost varies
Serves 200–300

Ham Lake
Ham Lake Senior Center
15544 Central Ave. NE
Ham Lake, MN 55304
612-434-0455
Third Friday in October and
second Friday in January,
4–8 p.m., all you can eat
Tickets at door, $7.50 adults,
$3.50 children under 12.
Serves 400–500
Note: All prepared by non-
Norwegian cook, Vie Johnson.
Meal consists of lutefisk, boiled
spuds, green beans, carrots,
rutabagas.

Hanska
Zion Lutheran Church
211 Summit Ave.
Hanska, MN 56041
507-439-6201
Last Saturday in October,
4–8 p.m.
Tickets at door, $9–$9.50
Serves 400

Harmony
Greenfield Lutheran Church
235 Main Ave. S.
Harmony, MN 55939
507-886-3272
Biannual. Next dinner will be
October or November 1997,
11–5 p.m. Served family style.
Tickets at door or advance, $8.50,
call church
Serves 1,000
Note: Servers dress in Norwe-
gian costumes.

Hotterdahl
Salem Lutheran Church
Box 128
Hotterdahl, MN 56552
218-962-3213
October, 5–7 p.m.
Tickets $8
Serves 300

Hutchinson
Our Savior's Lutheran Church
800 Bluff St.
Hutchinson, MN 55350
Fall, 4:30–8 p.m.
Tickets at door, $8 call
 Mary Givens, 612-587-4200 or
 234-7005
Serves 300
Note: "It is a German Lutheran
 Church!"

Jackson
*Our Savior's Evangelical
 Lutheran Church*
614 Logan Ave.
Jackson, MN 56143
January, 5 and 6:30 p.m.
Tickets at door and two to three
 weeks in advance, $6.50,
 contact the church.
Serves 100–150

Kasson
St. John's Lutheran Church
301 Fifth Ave. NW
Kasson, MN 55944-1098
Fourth Thursday in October,
 11 a.m. until all are served.
Tickets at door, $9
Serves 2,000

Kellcher
Our Savior's Lutheran Church
Kellcher, MN 56650
218-647-8364
First Thursday in December,
 5–7 p.m.
Tickets $7.50
Serves 400

Lakeville
Christiania Lutheran Church
26691 Pillsbury Ave.
Lakeville, MN 55044-9716
Fourth Saturday in October,
 4:30, 6 and 7:30 p.m.
Reservations recommended. Sale
 at church on second Sunday in
 October or contact church, $9
 last year, might change.
Serves 600

St. John's Lutheran Church
8748 210th St. W.
Lakeville, MN 55044-0955

Second Saturday of November,
 4:30, 6, and 7:30 p.m.
Tickets in advance, $9.50 adults,
 $5 children under 12, contact
 church
Serves 630

Lester Prairie
Bethel Lutheran Church
77 Lincoln Ave.
Lester Prairie, MN 55354
Last Sunday in October, 1–7 p.m.
Tickets at door, $10
Serves 850
Note: Served family style, all you
 can eat.

Little Falls
Bethel Lutheran Church
321 W. Broadway
Little Falls, MN 56345-1534
First Tuesday in December,
 4:30–8 p.m.
Tickets in advance, $8 adults, $3
 children under 12
Serves 525–600

Lindstrom
Hiram Lodge
Elm Street and Highway 8
PO Box 681
Lindstrom, MN 55045
First Saturday in December,
 4–7 p.m.
Tickets at door, $8
Serves 500–700

Mankato
Bethany Lutheran College
734 Marsh St.
Mankato, MN 56001
A Thursday in mid-October
 beginning of mid-term break,
 4–7 p.m.
Tickets at door, $11
Serves 500
Note: All faculty and staff do
 preparation and serving. The
 last three years there has been
 a special table for selling
 Norwegian baked goods.

Mapleton
Medo Lutheran Church
Route 2, Box 53
Mapleton, MN 56065

A Sunday in November or
December, 1, 3, and 5 p.m.,
family style
Tickets in advance, $9.50 adults,
$4 children under 12, contact
church
Serves 350–400
Note: Servers dress in Norwe-
gian costume, tell jokes.

Marine on St. Croix
Christ Lutheran Church
P.O. Box 37
150 Fifth St.
Marine on St. Croix, MN 55047
February, 11:30 a.m.–1 p.m.
and 4:30–7 p.m.
Tickets at door, $12
Serves 600

Milaca
Trinity Lutheran Church
Milaca High School Cafeteria
735 SE Second St.
PO Box 131
Milaca, MN 56353
612-983-7206
Last Saturday in October,
5–8 p.m.
Tickets at door, $7.50 adults, $5
children under 13
Serves 700

Minneapolis
*American Swedish Institute in
Minneapolis*
2600 Park Ave.
Minneapolis, MN 55407-1090
First Monday in December,
12, 1, 2, and 4 p.m.
Tickets in advance, $10, go on
sale the first of November,
contact church
Serves 600

Bethlehem Lutheran Church
4100 Lyndale Ave. S.
Mineapolis, MN 55409-1499
Second Saturday in November,
4 and 6 p.m.
Reservations required, $9
contact the church
Serves 400
Note: Exclusively put on by high
school students and their

families. Kids make lefse. Kids
endure lutefisk to do their
mission work for the church.

Holy Trinity Lutheran Church
2730 E. 31st St.
Minneapolis, MN 55406
612-729-8358
Second Saturday in December,
2–6 p.m.
Reservations required, cost
varies, contact the church
Serves 400–600

Lebanon Lutheran Church
2014 E. 36th St.
Minneapolis, MN 55407
612-729-7356
Second Friday in November,
4–7 p.m., all you can eat
Tickets at door, $10
Serves 500–600
Note: They have had the dinner
for 50 years.

*Lutheran Church
of the Good Shepherd*
4803 France Ave.
Minneapolis, MN 55410
Earl Hillstrand, 612-884-7619
October and March, 3:30 and
7 p.m.
Tickets $11, reservations
required. Send check to
Norwegian Glee Club
21 W. 108 St.
Bloomington, MN 55431
Serves 500

*Mindekerken Norwegian
Lutheran Memorial Church*
924 E. 21st St.
Minneapolis, MN 55404
Third Saturday of November,
4–7 p.m.
Reservations encouraged, $10,
start selling in September,
mail to: PO Box 7320,
Minneapolis, MN 55407-0320
Serves 500

*Minnehaha Communion
Lutheran Church*
4101 37th Ave. S.
Minneapolis, MN 55406
Kathy Danz, 612-722-2392

First Saturday in November,
4, 5:15 and 6:30 p.m.
Reservations required, $10, call
in September
Serves 300–400
Note: Dinner served family style.
They sing a lutefisk song.

Mount Olivet Lutheran Church
5025 Knox Ave. S.
Minneapolis, MN 55419
First Friday in December,
3–7 p.m., buffet, all you can eat
Tickets at door, $10
Serves 1,800–2,000

Our Redeemer Lutheran Church
4000 28th Ave. S.
Minneapolis, MN 55406-3119
First Sunday in February,
4–6 p.m.
No reservations needed, contact
church if you want tickets
early
Tickets $9 adults, $17 a couple,
$6 children 6–12, under 6 free
Serves 175–200
Note: Momentos of heritage on
display. Meal consists of
Swedish meatballs, pickled
herring, lutefisk, rutabagas,
potatoes, gluge, cream pudding, lingonberries, lefse.

Nelson
Corral Supper Club
Nelson, MN 56355
Tuesday nights in December and
January, 5–9 p.m.
First come, first served, $7.50

New Hope
House of Hope Lutheran Church
4800 Boone Ave. N.
New Hope, MN 55428-4498
First Friday in November,
3:30–7:30 p.m.
Reservations required, about
$10, tickets on sale in early
October
Serves 650–750
Note: Served home style in bowls
on tables. They have piano
entertainment and a craft
and bake sale.

Northfield
Three Links Care Center
815 Forest Ave.
Northfield, MN 55057-1643
507-645-6611
Thursday before Thanksgiving
November, 4:30–7 p.m.
Tickets at door and in advance,
$10 adults, $5 children under
12
Serves 400
Note: The "Lost Norwegians," a
folk singing group, entertain.
Students at St. Olaf and staff
at care center serve. Room is
decorated with Swedish and
Norwegian trinkets. Craft sale
and homemade bulk lefse is
sold.

Plainview
Good Shepherd Lutheran Church
Highway 42
Plainview, MN 55964-0355
507-534-3675
October or November, 5:30–7 p.m.
Tickets at door or in advance, $9
Serves 65

Porter
Bethel Lutheran Church
PO Box 126
Porter, MN 56280
507-296-4658
First Friday in November,
4–7:30 p.m.
Tickets at door, $7–$8
Serves 500–550

Preston
Christ Lutheran Church
509 Kansas St.
Preston, MN 55965
507-765-2161
First or second Sunday in
December, every hour
11 a.m.–5 p.m.
Tickets in advance, $9
Serves 700–800

Red Lake Falls
Bethany Lutheran Church
1315 Sixth St. NE
Red Lake Falls, MN 56750
218-253-2589

Late October, 4–8 p.m.
Tickets $6
Serves 400

Richfield
*King Oscar's Scandinavian
   Restaurant*
1120 E. 66th St.
Richfield, MN 55423
612-869-8311
Tuesdays and Saturdays October
   through February, every day in
   December, 11 a.m. –8 p.m.
$10.25
Note: Music every night.

Rothsay
Rothsay Truck Stop and Cafe
544 Center St. N.
Rothsay, MN 56579
218-867-2197
Mondays Thanksgiving through
   Christmas, call for times
$5.95
Serves 50–60 each Monday

Sargeant
Evanger Lutheran Church
Route 1, Box 116
Sargeant, MN 55973
507-584-6629
Third Friday in October, MEA
   weekend, 11 a.m.–1 p.m.,
   5, 6, 7, and 7:30 p.m.
Reservations for evening meals,
   $9.50, tickets go on sale
   October 1
Serves 1,000–1,050
Note: First supper was held on
   November 13, 1930. Total meal
   cost: $143.53

Scandia
Elim Lutheran Church
Scandia Community Center
20971 Olinda Trail
Scandia, MN 55073
612-433-2723
Sponsored by Gammelgarden
   Museum
Third Thursday in November,
   12, 4 and 6 p.m.
Tickets in advance, $10, contact
   612-433-3430 or 433-5053, or
   Gammelgarden Museum
   9885 202 St.

Forest Lake, MN 55025
Serves 600–800

St. Louis Park
VFW
5605 W. 36th St.
Highway 100 and 36th Street
St. Louis Park, MN 55416
612-929-4144
November, 4–7:30 p.m.
Reservations and tickets, $10,
   call 612-473-8619.
Serves 250

St. Paul
*First Lutheran Church of
   St. Paul*
463 Maria Ave.
St. Paul MN 55106-4428
612-776-7210
Second Saturday in November,
   3, 4, and 5 p.m.
Reservations needed, $8–9, call
   the church
Serves 400–600

Gloria Dei Lutheran Church
700 S. Snelling Ave.
St. Paul, MN 55116-2297
Jim Johnson, 612-699-7635
Second Friday in December,
   6:30 p.m.
Tickets in advance, $10
Serves 300
Note: They have a program with
   jokes, sing lutefisk lament
   hymn song, and the St. Paul
   Winter Carnival royalty
   attend. Money is given to Boy
   and Girl Scouts.

Immanuel Lutheran Church
104 Snelling Ave. S.
St. Paul, MN 55105-1999
612-699-5560
Friday before Thanksgiving,
   5, 6, and 7 p.m.
Reservations, $11
Serves 900

St. Peter
Scandian Grove Lutheran Church
Route 3
St. Peter, MN 56082
507-246-5195

Last Saturday in October,
11 a.m.–1 and 4:30–8 p.m.
Tickets $8.50
Serves 1,000
Note: Past pastors attend the
dinner. Valet parking is
available.

Staples
Faith Lutheran Church
631 Third Ave.
Staples, MN 56479
218-894-1546
November election night,
5–7 p.m.
Tickets $8.50
Serves 600

Stillwater
Trinity Lutheran Church
115 N. Fourth St.
Stillwater, MN 55082
612-439-7400
First Thursday in November,
11 a.m., 12, 4, 5, 6, and 7 p.m.
Tickets in advance, $10, starting
second week in October
Serves 1,000–1,300

Sunberg
Hope Lutheran Church
Highways 9 and 104
Sunberg, MN 56289
612-366-3586
Last Saturday in October,
3–8 p.m.
Tickets at door, about $7.50
Serves 1,000

Thief River Falls
Oakridge Lutheran Church
Thief River Falls, MN 56701
218-523-4596
Third weekend in January,
4–8 p.m.
Tickets $6
Serves 350

Trinity Lutheran Church
N Fourth and Horace Avenue
Thief River Falls, MN 56701
218-681-1310
First Thursday in November,
5–8 p.m.
Tickets $6.50
Serves 600

Tofte
Zoar Lutheran Church
Hwy. 61, Box 2098
Tofte, MN 55615
218-663-7925
First weekend in November,
5–8 p.m.
Tickets $5
Serves 150

Tracy
Tracy Lutheran Church
64 Rowland St.
Tracy, MN 56175-1327
507-629-3563
Third Sunday in November,
4, 5:30, and 7 p.m.
Tickets in advance, $8.50 adults,
$4.25 children ages 6–10,
under 5 free
Note: Youths put whole dinner
together.

Two Harbors
Miller's Cafe
Highway 61
Two Harbors, MN 55616
218-834-2452
November 1 through Christmas,
all day
Tickets $9.95
Serves 40–50

Vining
Vining Lutheran Church
P.O. Box 38
Vining, MN 56588
218-769-4382
October, 5–7:30 p.m.
Tickets $8
Serves 300

Virginia
Gethsemane Lutheran Church
901 S. Fourth St.
Virginia, MN 55792
218-741-4961
First Tuesday in December,
11 a.m.–1 p.m. and 4:30–7 p.m.
Tickets at door, $7
Serves 600

White Bear Lake
*First Evangelical Lutheran
  Church*
Highway 61 and County Road F
White Bear Lake, MN
  55110-4252
612-429-5349
End of October or early Novem-
  ber, 4:30, 5:30, and 6:30 p.m.
Reservations advised, call church
  for cost.
Serves 600–700

Willmar
Vinje Lutheran Church
1101 SW Willmar Ave.
Willmar, MN 56201
612-235-1441
First Tuesday in November,
  4–8 p.m.
Tickets at door, $7.50
Serves 800
Note: Music is performed in the
  sanctuary before seating.

Worthington
First Lutheran Church
1200 Fourth Ave.
Worthington, MN 56187
507-376-6148
First week in December, 2:30 and
  5:30 p.m.
Tickets at door, $8 adults, $4
  students under grade 12

MONTANA
Big Fork
Bethany Lutheran Church
Box 398
Big Fork, MT 59911
406-837-4387
Second Saturday in November,
  call church for times
Tickets in advance $8.50
Serves 600
Note: Started in 1918 as a
  "Welcome Home" dinner
  for men in the service.

Bozeman
Fjelldal 4-543
Senior Center
807 N. Tracy Ave.
Bozeman, MT 59715
Ron Glock, 406-587-4360

Last Sunday in October,
  12:30 and 2:15 p.m.
Tickets in advanced, starting two
  weeks before, $9 adults, $5
  children
Serves 350
Note: Amusing myths and folk
  tales are told at the dinner.

Cutbank
St. Paul Lutheran Church
602 E. Main St.
Cutbank, MT 59427
406-873-2794
First Sunday in December
Tickets in advance, starting in
  November, $8
Serves 700–800
Note: Potato flakes for lefse are
  bought from Sam's Club in
  Great Falls because they seem
  to be better than local potato
  flakes.

Fort Peck
Gateway Inn and Supper Club
Box 41
Fort Peck, MT 59223
406-526-9988
Call restaurant for dates, cost,
  and lutefisk serving times.

Great Falls
Lodsen 4-138
Lodsen Lodge Hall
1314 Seventh St. S.
Box 1307
Great Falls, MT 59403
Eloda Sangray, 406-452-5340
First Sunday in November,
  12–6 p.m.
Tickets at door, $8 adults, $4
  children 6–12
Serves 700–900

Havre
First Lutheran Church
303 Sixth Ave., P.O. Box 66
Havre, MT 59501
406-265-5881
First Saturday in February,
  12–6 p.m.
Tickets at door, $8 adults, $4
  children under 18
Serves 700

Helena
Hovedstad 4-528
Neighborhood Center
Helena, MT 59601
Gloria Hodge, 406-442-9704
Second Saturday in November,
5 p.m.
Tickets in advance, starting in
October, $7.50
Serves 750–1,000

Kalispell
Fedreheinmen 4-140
Sons of Norway Hall
347 First Ave. E.
Box 1292
Kalispell, MT 59903
Ed Prestegard, 406-257-3305
Last Saturday in October,
4–8 p.m.
Tickets at door, $8.50
Serves 425

Lewiston
Snofjeldedd 4-531
VFW
Lewiston, MT 59457
406-538-5354
Second Sunday in February,
6 p.m.
Cost varies
Serves only members, spouses
and special guests.

Libby
Norhaven 4-536
Hatlin Hall
165 Garden Rd.
Libby, MT 59923
David Gustad, 406-293-4687
February, 4 and 6 p.m.
Tickets in advance, starting in
January, $9 adults, $4.50
children
Serves 200

Missoula
Immanual Lutheran Church
830 South Ave. W.
Missoula, MT 59801
406-549-0736
First Saturday in December,
5 p.m.
Tickets $8.50
Serves 400–500

Sidney
Sidney 4-489
Sons of Norway Lodge
489 714 E. Main
Sidney, MT 59270
Coy McMorris, 406-482-1259
December and May, 3–6 p.m.
Tickets in advance, starting in
November or April, $7.50
Serves 50

NEVADA
Reno
Hvite Fjell 151, Sons of Norway
Little Flower Church
Corner of Kietzke Lane and
Plumb
Reno, NV 89509
702-322-2255
First Saturday after first Tues-
day in December, 5–11 p.m.
Tickets at door, prefer minimum
donation of $10
Serves 150
Note: It is a Christmas dinner,
with dancing afterwards. A
person plays the accordion too.

NORTH DAKOTA
Alexander
Trinity Lutheran Church
Alexander, ND 58831
701-828-3385
First Sunday in October,
12:30–4:30 p.m.
Tickets $8
Serves 350

Almont
Almont Legion Hall
Main St.
Almont ND 58520
701-843-7032 or 710-843-7634
First Saturday in November,
2:30–9 p.m.
Tickets $8
Serves 800–1,000

Arnegard
PDQ Supper Club
501 N. Main St.
Arnegard, ND 58835
701-586-3580

Mid-November, call for serving
hours
Tickets $8
Serves 80–100

Bismarck
Sons of Norway Sverdurp 107
Trinity Lutheran Church
502 N. Fourth St.
Bismarck, ND 58501
701-663-5609
Last Saturday in January,
3–7:30 p.m.
Tickets at door, $8 adults, $4
children
Serves 1,000

Bottineau
First Lutheran Church
701 Main St.
Bottineau, ND 58318
701-228-2228
October through November,
4–7 p.m.
Tickets $7.50
Serves 500

Bowden
Bowden Lions Club
Bowden Community Center
Main St., Box 374
Bowden, ND 58418
701-962-3630
Second or third Saturday in
November, 5–7 p.m.
Tickets $7
Serves 200

Buffalo
Fingle/Maple Valley School
Buffalo Elementary School
400 North Dakota Ave. NW
Buffalo, ND 58011-0165
701-633-5207 or 701-633-5183
Last Sunday in October, 12–5
p.m.
Tickets $6.50
Serves 700

Carrington
Kvernes Lutheran Church
Carrington, ND 58421
701-674-3371
First or second Sunday in
December, 11 a.m.–12:30 p.m.
Free.

Serves members of congregation
only.

Cooperstown
Sons of Norway
Cooperstown Lodge Building
Main St., Box 623
Cooperstown, ND 58425
701-797-3464
First Sunday in December,
4–7 p.m.
Tickets $8
Serves 100–150

Crosby
Concordia Lutheran Church
301 Main St. NE
Box 66
Crosby, ND 58730
701-965-6074
Second Saturday in November,
11 a.m.–8 p.m.
Tickets $8
Serves 800–1,000

Devils Lake
St. Olaf Lutheran Church
Sixth Street and Sixth Avenue
Devils Lake, ND 58301
701-662-4911
October, 5–7 p.m.
Tickets $7
Serves 500

Fargo
Sons of Norway
Kringen Club
722 Second Ave. N.
Fargo, ND 58102
701-232-9222
Every seventh week,
10:45 a.m.–1:30 p.m.
Tickets $8
Serves 400–500

Randy's Restaurant North
2828 Broadway
Fargo, ND 58102
701-280-1231
November through December,
4–8 p.m. Mondays
Tickets $6.95
Serves several thousand
throughout season.

Note: There are three other Randy's Restaurants in Fargo that also do lutefisk dinners. Check the yellow pages for phone numbers.

Forman
Trinity Lutheran Church
410 Cedar Ave. W.
Forman, ND 58032
701-724-3349
Second Sunday in October, 3–7 p.m.
Tickets $8
Serves 400

Galesburg
Elm River Lutheran Church
Galesburg, ND
701-488-2515
February, 4–7 p.m.
Tickets $7
Serves 400

Grafton
Our Savior's Lutheran Church
525 Kittson Ave.
Grafton, ND 58237
701-352-1627
Saturday near Syttende Mai, 4:30–6:30 p.m.
Tickets $6.50 adults, $3 children
Serves 200

Grand Forks
Big Sioux Truck Stop
I-29 and 32nd Avenue South
Grand Forks, ND 58201
701-746-6584
December through January, 11 a.m.–10 p.m.
Tickets $6.50
Serves 1,200

Grand Forks
Sons of Norway: Gyda Varden Lodge
Grand Forks Civic Center
615 First Ave. N.
Grand Forks, ND 58201
701-772-3545
Last Sunday in October, 11 a.m.–2:30 p.m.
Tickets $8 adults, $4 children
Serves 400

Gwinner
Gustaf Adolf Lutheran Church
207 First St. SE
Gwinner, ND 58040
701-678-2552 or 701-678-2343
Last Sunday in October, 1–7 p.m.
Tickets $7.50
Serves 700

Jamestown
Trinity Lutheran Church
523 Fourth Ave. SE
Jamestown, ND 58401
701-252-2841
Last Wednesday in October, 4–7 p.m.
Tickets $7 adults, $3 children
Serves 700

Lakota
Sunlac Inn
Junction of Highways 1 and 2
Box 648
Lakota, ND 58344
701-247-2487
Early November, 11 a.m.
Tickets $6.75
Serves 100

Lisbon
Trinity Lutheran Church
418 Fifth Ave. W.
Lisbon, ND 58054
701-683-5841
First or second Sunday in November, 4–8 p.m.
Tickets $7 adults, $6.50 seniors
Serves 70

Mandan
First Lutheran Church
408 NW Ninth St.
Mandan, ND 58554
701-663-3594
Early October, 3:30–8 p.m.
Tickets $8
Serves 750

Max
Our Savior's Lutheran Church
504 Carvell St.
Max, ND 58759
701-679-2771
First or second Sunday in October, 1–6 p.m.

Tickets $8
Serves 600

Minot
Bethany Lutheran Church
215 Third Ave. SE
Minot, ND 58701
701-838-5196
First or second Thursday in
    December, 11 a.m.–7 p.m.
Tickets $8
Serves 1,000

Norsk Hostfest
Minot All Seasons Arena
State Fair Grounds
Minot, ND 58701
701-852-2368
Mid-October, 11 a.m.–7 p.m.
Tickets $8
Serves thousands

Sons of Norway-Thor 67
Moose Club
400 SW Ninth St.
Minot, ND 58701
701-838-8554
Last week in February,
    11 a.m.–7 p.m.
Tickets $8.50
Serves 1,000

Minot Moose Lodge
400 SW Ninth St.
Minot, ND 58701
701-838-6387 or 701-838-6200
November, 4–8 p.m.
Tickets $8.50
Serves 700–1,000

Zion Lutheran Church
218 SW First St.
Minot, ND 58701
701-852-1872
Last Friday in September,
    3–8 p.m.
Tickets $8.50
Serves 750–1,000

New Rockford
Eagles Club
Midstate Shrine Club
7 South Eighth St.
New Rockford, ND
701-947-2495

Near Thanksgiving,
    4:30–7:30 p.m.
Tickets $7
Serves 300

Newtown
Bethel Lutheran Church
284 Second St. N.
Newtown, ND 58763
701-627-4434
Fall, call for times and
    contribution amount
Serves 450

Park River
Park River Bible Camp
Park River, ND 58270
701-284-6795
Last Sunday in September,
    12–6 p.m.
Tickets $8
Serves 1,300

Ray
Ray Lutheran Church
216 Score St., Box 157
Ray, ND 58849
701-568-3371
End of October or early
    November, 5–8 p.m.
Tickets $7.50
Serves 300–400

Richland/Walcott
Richland Lutheran Church
6147 172 Ave. SE
Walcott, ND 58077
701-553-9123
Last Friday in October,
    12–8:30 p.m.
Tickets $8
Serves 1,000

Roseglen
Emmanuel Lutheran Church
Roseglen, ND 58775
701-743-4336
Last Sunday in September,
    3–7 p.m.
Tickets $8.50 adults,
    $3.50 children
Serves 500

Rugby
First Lutheran Church
202 SE Fourth St.
Rugby, ND 58368
701-776-5801
Early in November, 5–8 p.m.
Tickets $7.50
Serves 400

Hub Restaurant
Junction of Highways 2 and 3
Box 285
Rugby, ND 58368-0285
701-776-5807
Near Christmas, 9:30 a.m.–2 p.m.,
   buffet; and Lent, 5–9:30 p.m
Buffet, $6.95 and Lent, $4.95
Serves 300

St. Thomas
St. John's Lutheran Church
Main St.
St. Thomas, ND 58276
701-257-6799
Second or third Sunday in
   November, 11:30–3 p.m.
Tickets $7.50 adults, $3 children
Serves 300

Stanley
American Lutheran Church
403 First St. SW
Stanley, ND 58784
701-628-2550
October or November, 4–7 p.m.
Tickets $8
Serves 400

Thompson
Walle Lutheran Church
746 Ninth St.
Box 326
Thompson, ND 58278
701-599-2382
Early in November, 5–7:30 p.m.
Tickets $8
Serves 300

Towner
Zion Lutheran Church
107 Fourth Ave. SW
Towner, ND 58788-0569
701-537-5654
Last Sunday in October, 4–7 p.m.
Tickets $7.50 adults, $4 children
Serves 500

Valley City
Eagle's Lodge
345 12th Ave. NE
Valley City, ND 58072
701-845-2192
Second Tuesday in November,
   6–10 p.m.
Tickets $7
Serves 200–300

Velva
Oak Valley Lutheran Church
400 N. Main St.
Velva, ND 58790
701-338-2642
Last Sunday in October, 2–7 p.m.
Tickets $8.50 adults,
   $3.50 children
Serves 500

Walcott
Walcott Lutheran Church
537 Third St.
Walcott, ND 58077
701-469-2183
Third Sunday in October,
   12–6 p.m.
Tickets $8
Serves 650

Richland Lutheran Church
Walcott, ND 58077
701-553-8874
Last Friday in October,
   12–8 p.m.
Tickets $8 adults, $3 under 12
Serves 800–1100

Walhalla
Walhalla Lutheran Church
Walhalla, ND 58282
701-549-2540
Last Sunday in October, 1–6 p.m.
Tickets $8.50 adults, $4 children
Serves 750

Washburn
First Lutheran Church
709 Fifth Ave., Box 218
Washburn, ND 58577
710-462-3775 or 710-462-3774
Last Sunday in October, 2–7 p.m.
Tickets $7.50
Serves 900

Williston
First Lutheran Church
916 Main St.
Williston, ND 58801-5398
701-572-6363
Third week in February,
    11 a.m.–7 p.m.
Tickets $8 adults, $3 children
Serves 3,000

OREGON
Eugene
Sonja 38, Sons of Norway
Sons of Norway Hall
1836 Alder St.
Eugene, OR 97401
503-344-1064
Last Saturday and Sunday in
    January; Saturday, 3, 5, and
    7 p.m., Sunday, 1, 3, 5, and
    7 p.m.
Tickets $10
Serves 700
Comments: "Once you're done
    eating turkey, think about
    eating lutefisk."

Medford
Roguedalen 143, Sons of Norway
Westminster Presbyterian
    Church
2000 Oakwood Dr.
Medford, OR 97504
541-773-8274
First or second Saturday in
    November, 6–10 p.m.
Tickets $12, contact:
    Levone Jensen
    1074 Galls Creek Rd.
    Gold Hill, OR 97525-9704
    541-855-9830
Serves 120–140

Portland
Grieg 15, Sons of Norway
Norse Hall
111 NE 11th Ave.
Portland, OR 97232
503-236-3401
Second Sunday in November,
    12:30, 2, 3:30 p.m., all you
    can eat.
Tickets $15, send self-addressed
    stamped envelope to

Edna Koroch,
7532 SE Tibbetts
Portland, OR 97206-1846
503-771-2689
Serves 600

SOUTH DAKOTA
Aberdeen
Bethlehem Lutheran Church
215 Fourth Ave. SE
Aberdeen, SD 57401
605-225-9740
November date varies, call
    church for times.
Tickets $6.50
Note: They call it "Norway
    Night."

Baltic
Baltic Cafe
201 St. Olaf Ave.
Baltic, SD 57003
605-529-5429
Served often during the year for
    the "good ole boys." Call for
    dates and serving hours.
Tickets $6.95

Beresford
Betty's Place
104 N. Third. St.
Beresford, SD 57004
605-763-5006
November date varies, Sundays in
    January, call for serving hours
Tickets $9.95

Brookings
Casper's Cafe
420 S. Main Ave.
Brookings, SD 57006
605-692-7240
Fall date varies, call for serving
    times.
Tickets $7.95

Fjordland 508/Sons of Norway
Brookings County Agriculture
    Building
102 Fourth St. W.
Brookings, SD 57006
605-697-6706 or Dora Nelson,
    605-692-5576
November, members and guests
    only, call for times.
Tickets $7.95

Clark
St. Paul's Lutheran Church
301 S. Smith St.
Clark, SD 57225
605-532-3784
October date varies, call for
    times
Tickets $8

Lake Preston
North Preston Church
605-847-4545
January date varies, call church
    for times.
Tickets $10

Langford
Langford High School
Oak St., PO Box 127
Langford, SD 57454
605-493-6454
Fall date varies, call for times
Tickets $9

Mitchell
Fedrelandet 579/Sons of Norway
Chef Louie's Restaurant
601 E. Haven's St.
Mitchell, SD 57301
Sherry Stilley, 605-996-3595
Second Saturday in November,
    6:30 p.m.
Cost varies

Kiwanis Club
Kiwanis Club at Holiday Inn
Mitchell, SD 57301
605-996-5556
January date varies,
    call for times
Tickets $8.50

Pierre
Lutheran Memorial Church
320 E. Prospect, across from the
    capitol
Pierre, SD 57501
605-224-8608
February date varies, held
    during Legislative session,
    call church for times.
Tickets $7.50

Renner
Renner's Lutheran Church
Box 52
Renner, SD 57055
605-338-7120
November date varies, call
    church for times
Tickets $9

Sioux Falls
Norse Glee Club and Auxiliary
Nordic Hall
218 W. 13th St.
Sioux Falls, SD 57102
605-332-9750
Third Friday in October and
    November, call for times
Tickets $7

Sioux Falls/Beresford
Yesterday's Cafe
Highways 29 and 46
605-763-5300
Mondays in November through
    February, call for serving
    hours
Tickets $8.95

Viborg
Kountry Kookin' Restaurant
106 Main St.
Viborg, SD 57070
605-326-5516
November through January, call
    for serving hours
Tickets $7.50

White
Pioneer Lutheran Church
Box 6
White, SD 57276
605-629-6801
February date varies, call for
    times
Tickets $8

Yankton
Yesterday's Cafe
2102 Broadway St.
Yankton, SD 57037
605-665-4383
November, call for hours and
    cost.
Note: They serve "luscious
    Lutheran lefse."

TEXAS
Cranfills Gap
Cranfills Gap High School
School Rd., PO Box 67
Cranfills Gap, TX 76637
817-597-2225
First Saturday in December,
  4:30, 5:30, 6:30, 7:30 p.m.
Tickets $10–11, contact
  Barbara Epley
  PO Box 76
  Cranfills Gap, TX 76637
  817-597-2531
Serves 600–800
Note: It has been a fund-raiser
  for the school for more than 30
  years. Girls serve dinner and
  boys park the cars. Turkey and
  dressing are also served. Many
  people bring food to share.

UTAH
North Ogden
Odin 101, Sons of Norway
Ascension Lutheran Church
1105 N. Washington Blvd.
North Ogden, UT 84404
801-782-2810
First Saturday in November,
  4, 5, and 6 p.m.
Reservations, $10 adults, $8 se-
  niors over 65, $4 children
Serves 300
Note: Also serves lefse,
  krumkake, and other
  Norwegian goodies.

WASHINGTON
Aberdeen
Trinity Lutheran Church
201 North I St.
Aberdeen, WA 98520
360-532-9093
Mid-December, call church for
  times
Tickets at door, $12
Serves 150

Bellingham
Wergeland 21
Sons of Norway Hall
1419 N. Forest St.
Bellingham, WA 98226
360-733-6618

First weekend in December, call
  for time
Tickets $15
Serves 250

Bothell
Bothell 106
Sons of Norway Hall
23905 Bothell-Everett Hwy.
PO Box 492
Bothell, WA 98041
First Saturday in December, call
  for time
Tickets at door, $12
Serves 1,200

Bremerton
Oslo Lodge 35
Sons of Norway Hall
1018 18th Ave.
Bremerton, WA 98310
360-375-1503
First Sunday in November, call
  for times
Tickets at door, $10
Serves 1,200
Note: They have a bazaar at the
  same time.

Centralia
Skjonndal Lodge 127
Fords Prairie Grange
2640 Reynolds Ave.
PO Box 31
Centralia, WA 98531
Clayton Anderson, 360-330-2176
Sunday in early November, call
  for times
Tickets at door $12.50
Serves 130

Everett
Normanna 3, Sons of Norway
Sons of Norway Hall
2725 Oakes St.
Everett, WA 98201
206-252-0291
Third Sunday in October, 12–4
  p.m.
Tickets $10–12
Serves 600–900
Note: Served family style, with
  meatballs, flat bread, potatoes,
  lefse.

Gig Harbor
Peninsula Lutheran Church
6509 38th Ave. NW
Gig Harbor, WA 98335
206-851-3511
Last Friday and Saturday in
    October, call for times
Tickets at door, $10
Serves 1,400

Hoquiam
Grays Harbor 4
Sons of Norway Hall
717 Randall
Aberdeen, WA 98520
360-532-3260
Sunday in mid-November, call
    for times
Tickets $11
Serves 400

Kelso
Briedablik 27, Sons of Norway
Sons of Norway Hall
224 Catlin St. W.
Kelso, WA 98626
360-425-7013
Second Sunday in January,
    12:30, 1:30, 3, and 4 p.m.
    Served family style.
Tickets $12, contact:
    Robert Fristad
    1005 N. Sixth Ave.
    Kelso, WA 98626
    360-423-7789
Serves 500
Note: There is accordion music
    and Scandinavian songs are
    sung.

Kennewick
Sol-land Lodge 86
First Lutheran Church
418 N. Yelm St.
Kennewick, WA 98336
509-783-6108
Friday in mid-November, call for
    times
Tickets at door, $10
Serves 300
Note: They have a craft display
    and demonstration and a raffle.

Kent/Auburn
Vesterdalen Lodge 2-131
Messiah Lutheran Church
Fourth and H Street
PO Box 99
Auburn, WA 98071
206-833-5280
Late October, call for times
Tickets at door, $14
Serves 900

Olympia
Hovedstad Lodge 94
Women's Club
1002 Washington
PO Box 10194
Olympia, WA 98506
360-753-9421
Saturday in early November, call
    for times
Tickets at door, $8.50
Serves 250, members only

Port Angeles
Olympic Lodge 37
Scandia Hall
131 W. Fifth St.
Port Angeles, WA 98362
360-452-2993
Saturday in early November, call
    for times
Tickets at door, $9.50
Serves 300
Note: They teach folk dance from
    3–7 on day of dinner.

Poulsbo
First Lutheran Church
18920 Fourth Ave. NE
Poulsbo, WA 98370
360-779-2622
Third Saturday in October, call
    for times
Tickets at door, $11
Serves 1,300
Note: They have been doing
    lutefisk dinners for at least 83
    years.

Seattle
Norwegian Male Chorus
Leif Erickson Hall
2245 NW 57th St.
Seattle, WA 98107

November or December, call for
 times
Tickets $10, for members and
 guests only
Serves 100

Spokane
Tordenskjold Lodge 5
Sons of Norway Hall
N. 6710 Country Homes Blvd.
Spokane, WA 99208
509-326-9211
January, call for times
Tickets $10
Serves 600

Stanwood
Stanwood Lions Club
Stanwood High School Cafeteria
7400 272nd St. NW
Stanwood, WA 98292
360-629-2167
Last Sunday in October,
 11 a.m.–5 p.m.
Tickets at door, $11–12
Serves 1,300
Note: Always gets fish from
 Poulsbo, Wash. Serves about
 2,200 lbs. of lutefisk, 500 lbs.
 of meatballs, and 1,000 lbs.
 of potatoes.

Tacoma
Normanna Lodge Hall
1106 S. 15th St.
Tacoma, WA 98405
360-876-4198
Second Sunday in October,
 11 a.m.–4 p.m.
Tickets at door, $10
Serves 600
Note: They have a bazaar at the
 same time.

Vancouver
Columbia Lodge 58
Sons of Norway Hall
2400 Grant
Vancouver, WA 98664
360-695-8721
Second Sunday in October, call
 for times
Tickets in advance, $12
Serves 200

Yakima
Odin Lodge 41
Masonic Center
510 N. Nachees Ave.
Yakima, WA 98901
509-457-6143
First Saturday in December, call
 for times
Tickets at door, $9.50
Serves 400
Note: They also serve
 rømmegrøt.

WISCONSIN
Appleton
Norse Valley Lodge 5-491,
 Sons of Norway
Columbus Club
2531 N. Richmond St.
Appleton, WI 54914
Mary Lovdahl, 414-734-4485
First Sunday in November,
 5–7 p.m.
Reservations required, $9.50
Serves 200
Note: Entertainment is provided.

Ashland
Birkebeiner Lodge 5-611,
 Sons of Norway
Good Shephard Lutheran
 Church
311 13th St.
Ashland, WI 54806
First week in November,
 4–7 p.m.
Tickets $8, call Edith Mahnke,
 715-682-4743
Serves 200
Note: The cook, Joy, sings "Just a
 Little Lefse" and "The Lutefisk
 Lament" while she cooks the
 fish. There are Norwegian
 pastries for dessert.

Barnevold
Barnevold Lutheran Church
503 Swiss Lane
Barnevold, WI 53507
608-924-8621
Last Saturday in October,
 1–7 p.m.
Tickets at door, $10
Serves 1,000

Beldenville
Our Savior's Lutheran Church
W5352 County Rd. N
Beldenville, WI 54003
715-273-4570
Last Thursday in October,
 2–7 p.m.
Tickets at door, bus loads must
 call in advance and arrive by
 1 p.m. to be served first.
Tickets $9
Serves 1,300
Note: Dining room is decorated
 in Scandinavian decor, and the
 servers are all in red vests and
 red caps. Talented church
 members provide entertainment for guests waiting to eat.

Black Earth
Vermont Lutheran Church
Highway 78 on
 Vermont Church Road
Black Earth, WI 53515
608-767-2247
Third Saturday in October,
 11 a.m.–7 p.m.
Tickets in advance, $11
Serves 1,200
Note: They serve *rømmegrøt* and
 bondepike for desserts.

Blair
First Lutheran Church
419 S. Urberg Ave.
Blair, WI 54616
608-989-2166
First Saturday in November,
 11 a.m.–8 p.m.
Tickets at door, $8
Serves 1,700
Note: There are Norwegian
 pastries for dessert.

Boaz
Five Points Lutheran Church
Route 1
Blue River, WI 53518
608-536-3877
4th Saturday in October,
 11 a.m.–2 p.m. and 4–8 p.m.
Tickets at door, $8.50
Serves 1,000
Note: Servers all wear
 Norwegian hats and aprons.

Cadott
Big Drywood Lutheran Church
2709 120th Ave.
Cadott, WI 54727
715-289-3608
Third Sunday in October,
 12–4 p.m
Tickets at door, $8.50, all you can
 eat
Serves 700

Chippewa Falls
Chippewa Masonic Lodge
650 Bridgewater Ave.
Chippewa Falls, WI 54729
715-723-6341
Fourth Thursday in October,
 4–7 p.m.
Tickets at door, $8, but may vary
Serves 300

Clear Lake
Moe Lutheran Church
451 30th St.
Clear Lake, WI 54005
715-263-2990
Third Sunday in October,
 12–4 p.m., family style
Tickets at door, $10
Serves 400

DeForest
Christ Lutheran Church
220 S. Main St.
DeForest, WI 53532
608-846-3558
Second Saturday in November,
 11 a.m.–7 p.m.
Tickets at door, $9.50
Serves 1,500

Ettrick
*North Beaver Creek Lutheran
 Church*
R.R. #1
Ettrick, WI 54627
608-525-2406
Last Sunday in October,
 11 a.m.–7 p.m.
Tickets at door, $8
Serves 1,200–1,600

Eau Claire
Burgundy's Restaurant
at Ramada Inn
1202 W. Clairmont Ave.
Eau Claire, WI 54701
715-834-3181
Tuesdays and Thursdays in
    January, 5–8:30 p.m.,
    Norwegian buffet.
Tickets $9.25
Serves 100

Holmen
Drugan's Supper Club
W7665 Sylvester Rd.
Holmen, WI 54636
608-526-4144
Sundays, October through
    February, 11:30 a.m–4 p.m.
Tickets $8.95
Serves 200
Note: Served family style and all
    you can eat.

Iola
Iola Winter Carnival
Iola High School Commons
Iola, WI 54945
Gary Jacobson, 715-445-2490 or
    715-445-2620
First weekend in February,
    1–7 p.m. on Saturday
Tickets at door, $9
Serves 1,200–1,300
Note: Nicknames for the
    husband and wife cooks are
    "Codmother" and "Codfather."

Northland Lutheran Church
N9880 Hwy. 49
Iola, WI 54945
715-445-2956
Third Saturday in October,
    1–8 p.m.
Tickets at door, $9
Serves 1,000
Note: "Codmother" and
    "Codfather" cook here, too.

Janesville
Nordland Lodge 5-544
Sons of Norway
418 W. Milwaukee St.
Janesville, WI 53545

Hjalmer Hanson, 608-752-5600
Second Saturday in November,
    11 a.m.–7 p.m.
Tickets at door or advance, $10,
    call 608-884-3286
Serves 300–350

La Crosse
Our Redeemer Lutheran Church
2135 Weston St.
La Crosse, WI 54601
608-788-0242
First Sunday in October,
    11 a.m.–3 p.m. and 4–7 p.m.
Tickets encouraged, $7, call the
    church
Serves 250

Madison
Burke Lutheran Church
5720 Portage Rd.
Madison, WI 53704
608-244-8486
First Saturday in November,
    11 a.m.–2 p.m. and 4–7 p.m.
Tickets at door, $8.50
Serves 1,200
Note: They serve cranberry sauce
    made from scratch. They go to
    the cranberry marshes in
    Warrens, Wis., and pick their
    own berries and make the
    sauce themselves.

Idun Lodge 5-074,
*   Sons of Norway*
Norway Center
2262 Winnebago St.
Madison, WI 53704
608-249-6329
Fourth Saturday in October,
    11 a.m.–7 p.m.
Tickets at door, $10
Serves 450–550
Note: Guests are treated
    occasionally to an impromptu
    concert of Norwegian music
    provided by the men who
    prepare the lutefisk.

Lakeview Lutheran Church
4001 Mandrake Rd.
Madison, WI 53704
608-244-6181
First Friday in November,
  11 a.m.–8 p.m.
Tickets at door or advance, $8.75,
  starting one month in advance
Note: Everything is home-cooked.

Merrill
Our Savior's Lutheran Church
300 Logan St.
Merrill, WI 54452
715-536-5813
First Thursday in November,
  11 a.m.–1 p.m. and 4–8 p.m.
Tickets at door, $8 adults, $4
  children 6–12, under 6 free
Serves 800
Note: Our congregation is mostly
  German and Italian.

Mondovi
Blondie's Diner
130 N. Eau Claire St.
Mondovi, WI 54755
715-926-3456
Sundays starting around deer
  hunting season until
  Christmas, 11 a.m.–2 p.m.
Reservations recommended,
  $5.95
Serves 150

Mondovi Inn Restaurant
836 E. Main St.
Mondovi, WI 54755
715-926-3943
First Wednesday in December
9 a.m.–11 p.m.
Reservations: Not needed.
Tickets $8.95
Serves 300
Note: Dinner is served buffet
  style.

Valley Supper Club
S80 Golf Rd.
Mondovi, WI 54755
715-926-4913
Thanksgiving, Christmas, and
  possibly New Year's, 5–10 p.m.
Tickets $7.95, all you can eat,
  reservations recommended
Serves 150

Monona
Leske's Supper Club
6401 Monona Dr.
Monona, WI 53716
608-222-8646
Mondays, early November
  through January,
  11 a.m.–9 p.m.
Tickets $6.75
Serves 40–50 each Monday

Mount Sterling
Utica Lutheran Church
Hwy. 27, 3 miles north of Mount
  Sterling in Crawford County
608-734-3051
Third Saturday in October,
  11 a.m.–1:30 p.m.
  and 4:30–8 p.m.
Tickets at door, $7.50 adults,
  $3.75 children 6–12, under
  6 free
Serves 850

New Auburn
Bethel Dover Lutheran Church
148 E. Pine St.
New Auburn, WI 54757
715-237-2228
First Friday in October, 4:30–8
  p.m.
Tickets at door, $8 adults, $4
  children 4–12, under 4 is free
Serves 230
Note: They have a raffle in con-
  junction with the dinner.

Sundial Supper Club
A128 County Rd. SS
New Auburn, WI 54757
715-237-2365
Third Wednesday in October
  and second Wednesday in
  November, 4–9 p.m.
Tickets $10
Serves about 100 each night

Orfordville
Orfordville Lutheran Church
210 N. Main St.
Orfordville, WI 53576
608-879-2575
Second Saturday in October,
  11 a.m.–7 p.m.
Tickets at door, $8.50 adults,
  $4.50 children 6–12

Note: The servers wear
Norwegian costumes.

Osceola
West Immanuel Lutheran Church
447 180th St.
Osceola, WI 54020
715-294-2936
Second Saturday in November,
11 a.m.–3 p.m. and 4–8:30 p.m.,
served family style
Tickets at door, $10
Serves 1,000

Osseo
Chief Inn Supper Club
3½ miles north of Osseo
on Hwy. 53
Osseo, WI 54758
715-597-2660
Sundays, October through
December, 11 a.m.–4 p.m.
Tickets $6.95, but may vary
Serves 100

Norske Nook Restaurant
West Seventh Street
Osseo, WI 54758
715-597-3069 or 715-597-3688
Call restaurant for dates,
10 a.m.–4 p.m.
Tickets $9, may vary

Rice Lake
Norske Nook Restaurant
2900 Pioneer Ave.
Rice Lake, WI 54868
715-234-1733
First Sunday in November,
December, and January,
11 a.m.–8 p.m.
Tickets $8.95 per plate
or $9.95 all you can eat.
Serves 400

Rio
Bonnet Prairie Lutheran Church
N3694 Old F Rd.
Rio, WI 53960
414-992-3200
First Saturday in November,
11 a.m.–2 p.m. and 4–7 p.m.
Tickets at door, $8
Serves 200

Rubicon
St. Olaf Lutheran Church
W653 Roosevelt Rd.
Rubicon, WI 53078
414-474-7042
First Wednesday in December,
3:30-8:30 p.m.
Tickets at door or advance, $8,
call church
Serves 750–800
Note: Church is very proud of
their Norwegian heritage and
traditions.

Strum/Trempealeau County
Bruce Valley Lutheran Church
6 miles South of Strum, Wis., on
County Highway D
715-695-3247
Second Sunday in October,
11 a.m.–3 p.m.
Tickets at door, $6.50
Serves 400
Note: The lutefisk is a fund-
raiser to keep the church open
during restoration.

Sturgeon Bay
H.R. Holand 5-549/
Sons of Norway
Bay View Lutheran Church
340 W. Maple Ave.
Sturgeon Bay, WI 54235
Second Friday in November,
5 p.m.
Tickets $10, call Lorraine
Selvick, 414-743-9600
Serves 150

Superior
Concordia Lutheran Church
1708 John Ave.
Superior, WI 54880
715-395-3762
First Friday in November,
4–7 p.m.
Tickets at door, $8
Serves 400–800
Comments: "This last dinner,
1995, was the biggest in a long
time. The lutefisk is donated.
Otherwise, they'd lose their
shirts!"

Viroqua
Viroqua Eagles Club
216 S. Rock St.
Viroqua, WI 54665
608-637-2707
First Saturday in December,
5–8 p.m., served buffet style
Tickets at door, $6
Serves 250–300

West Salem
Our Savior's Lutheran Church
359 N. Leonard St.
West Salem, WI 54669
608-786-0030
First Saturday in November,
3:30–8:30 p.m.
Tickets at door, $8
Serves 850–900

Westby
Our Savior's Lutheran Church
306 S. Main St.
Westby, WI 54667
608-634-4871
First Saturday in February,
11 a.m.–2 p.m. and 4–8 p.m.
Tickets at door, $8
Serves 500–1,000

Wind Lake
Norway Lutheran Church
6321 Heg Park Rd.
Wind Lake, WI 53185
414-895-2281
Second Friday in February,
12 noon for senior citizens,
6 and 7:30 p.m.
Tickets in advance, $13.50 for
seniors at noon dinner,
$15 for evening dinners,
call Donna Hanson at
414-534-3862 or Joanne
Jacobson, 414-534-6867
Serves 1,000
Note: Men and women wear
costumes during the dinner.
It is the oldest Norwegian
Lutheran church in the
United States.

CANADA

ALBERTA
Calgary
Vahalla 4-341
Scandinavian Center
739 20th Ave. NW
Calgary, ALTA T2M-1E2
Roy Swanberg, 403-287-3199
First Saturday in February, call
for times
Tickets in advance, starting two
weeks prior to dinner, $13
members, $15 non-members

Camrose
Ronning 4-504
Kingman Hall
Kingman, ALTA T0B 2M0
Pres. Lloyd Reed, 403-672-0021
First Friday in December,
4:30 p.m.
Tickets at door, $13–16
Serves 800
Comments: "The lutefisk capital
of the world!"

Claresholm
Hamar 4-345
Community Center
Claresholm, ALTA T0L 0T0
403-625-3774 or 403-625-2435
Last Saturday in January,
5:30 p.m., dinner and dance
Tickets before Christmas, $8
members, $16 non-members
Serves 300–350

Edmonton
Soglyt 4-143
Hosanna Lutheran Church
9009 163 St.
Edmonton, ALTA T5R 2N8
403-425-8261
Third Saturday in January,
7 p.m.
Tickets $16.50
Serves 160

Grand Prairie
Northern Lights 4-493
Lake Saskatoon Hall
Box 488
Wembley, ALTA T0H 3S0

Harold Kjemhus, 403-532-5673
or 403-766-3118
Last Sunday in November,
4–7 p.m.
Tickets in advance, $12
Serves 250

Lethbridge
Solsyd 603
Scandinavian Hall
229 12C St. N.
Lethbridge, ALTA
Andrew Alm, 403-320-5312
Last Sunday in October, 5 p.m.
Tickets in advance starting two
weeks before, $12
Serves 160–180

Medicine Hat
Skjenna 4-605
Folk Arts Center
First St.
Medicine Hat, ALTA T1A 0A5
Pres. Olga Perrier, 403-527-9838
Fourth Thursday in December,
6–10 p.m.
Tickets at door, cost of fish to
members, and then members
provide rest of the meal
Serves 26

Red Deer
Aspelund 4-571
United Church basement
Red Deer, ALTA
403-346-7670
Dates and time varies
Advanced tickets required, $15
Serves 150

Wetas Rawin
Normanna 4-595
Central Community Hall
Gwynne, ALTA
Karen Greenwall, 403-352-7695
Third Saturday in January,
6:30–7:30 p.m.
Tickets in advance starting two
weeks before, $15
Serves 100

BRITISH COLUMBIA
Castlegar
Nordic 76
Sandman Hotel
1944 Columbia Ave.
Castlegar, BC C1N 2W7
Alyse Mathisen, 604-352-9388
604-365-8444
Second weekend in December,
call for times
Tickets in advance, $25 mem-
bers, $28 non-members
Serves 100

Dawson
Dawson Creek 79
1513 113th Ave.
Dawson, BC V1G 224
604-782-9157
First Sunday in December, 4 p.m.
Tickets at door, $8
Serves 70
Note: They do it for a fun
Christmas dinner.

Kamloops
Heimdal 141,
    Leif Erickson 93 Lodge
IOOF Hall
Battle St.
Kamloops, BC V2C 5E5
604-573-4363
Third Saturday in November,
7 p.m. entertainment and
dancing follow
Tickets in advance, starting two
months before
Serves 120

Maple Ridge
Golden Ears 137
Golden Ears/Rusken Hall
96th Avenue at 284th Street
Maple Ridge, BC
604-826-6501
Last Saturday in November,
6:30 p.m.
Tickets in advance, $15 includes
entertainment
Serves 110

Prince George
Rondane 71
Location varies
Prince George, BC
604-962-7654
Third Saturday in October,
   6:30 p.m.
Tickets in advance, $20
Serves 40–50

Summerland
Scandinavian Club
Senior Drop In Center
9710 Brown St.
Summerland, BC V0H 1Z0
604-494-9377
First Saturday in December,
   6 p.m.
Tickets in advance, $12
Serves 100–150

Vancouver
Sleipner 8
Lodge Hall
6540 Thomas St.
Vancouver, BC V5E 4B7
604-522-5950
Usually first Sunday in
   December, 3 or 5 p.m.
Tickets in advance, starting one
   month before, $17

Victoria
Eidsvold 53
Eidsvold Lodge
1110 Hillside Ave.
Victoria, BC V8T 2A7
604-386-9812
Last Saturday in November, 6:30
   p.m.
Tickets in advance, $15

SASKATCHEWAN
North Battlefield
Nisse 4-567
United Church Hall
Third Avenue
North Battlefield, SASK
   S9A 3W1
President, 306-892-4300
Third Saturday in November,
   5:30–7:30 p.m.
Tickets in advance, starting
   three weeks before, $10
Serves 150–200
Note: Ladies in *bunads* parade
   the dinner with accordion
   music. Norwegian piano music
   is played throughout the
   dinner. They serve Norwegian
   pastries for dessert.

OOPS!
Did We Miss Your Annual Lutefisk Dinner?

If you want your annual lutefisk dinner listed in The Lutefisk Dinner
Directory, or if you want to make a change or correction in your current
listing, fill out the form below and fax it to: 612-926-0463.

Or mail the form to:

Conrad Henry Press, 5205 Knox Ave. S., Minneapolis, MN 55419-1041

State or province   City
_____

Church or organization
_____

Address (with zip or postal code)
_____

_____

Phone number (with area code)
_____

Date and time of dinner
_____

Serves how many?   Ticket price   Reservations required?
_____

Contact person (name and phone number)
_____

Comments about your dinner
_____

ORDER FORM

Please send me _____ copies of *The Last Word on Lutefisk*.
Please send me _____ copies of *The Last Word on Lefse*.

Fax orders: 612-926-0463
Telephone orders: Call toll free 1(888) LUTEFIS = 1(888) 588-3347.
Please have your credit card ready.
Postal orders: Conrad Henry Press
　　　　　　　　5205 Knox Ave. S.
　　　　　　　　Minneapolis, MN 55419-1041
Web site: http://www.lutefisk.com
E-mail: glegwold@lutefisk.com

*I understand that if I am not satisfied with these books, I may return
them for a full refund—no questions asked.*

Cost: $14.95 + tax + shipping.
Tax: Please add 7% ($1.05 for one book) if the book is shipped to
　　　Minneapolis, and 6.5% ($.97) if in Minnesota (outside of
　　　Minneapolis).
Shipping: $3.50 for the first book. For each additional book, add $.50
(U.S. only).

Please send the book(s) to:

Name: _____

Address: _____

City: _____　State: _____　Zip: _____

Payment: ❑ Check　❑ Credit card

Type of card: _____　Name on card: _____

Card number: _____　Exp. date: _____

Are you interested in Gary Legwold, author of *The Last Word on
Lutefisk* and *The Last Word on Lefse*, signing books and/or speaking at
your lutefisk dinner?

　If yes, give date and location of your dinner, contact person, and that
person's address and/or phone number.

_____

_____

_____

If Gary Legwold cannot attend your special lutefisk dinner, are you
interested in selling *The Last Word on Lutefisk* and *The Last Word on
Lefse* as part of your fund raiser?

Contact person and phone number: _____

_____

Did We Miss Your Annual Lutefisk Dinner?
Fill out the form on the other side of this page.